OSCAR
ROMERO

MODERN SPIRITUAL MASTERS
Robert Ellsberg, Series Editor

This series introduces the writing and vision of some of the great spiritual masters of the twentieth century. Along with selections from their writings, each volume includes a comprehensive introduction, presenting the author's life and writings in context and drawing attention to points of special relevance to contemporary spirituality.

Some of these authors found a wide audience in their lifetimes. In other cases recognition has come long after their deaths. Some are rooted in long-established traditions of spirituality. Others charted new, untested paths. In each case, however, the authors in this series have engaged in a spiritual journey shaped by the influences and concerns of our age. Such concerns include the challenges of modern science, religious pluralism, secularism, and the quest for social justice.

At the dawn of a new millennium this series commends these modern spiritual masters, along with the saints and witnesses of previous centuries, as guides and companions to a new generation of seekers.

Already published:
Dietrich Bonhoeffer (edited by Robert Coles)
Simone Weil (edited by Eric O. Springsted)
Henri Nouwen (edited by Robert A. Jonas)
Pierre Teilhard de Chardin (edited by Ursula King)
Charles de Foucauld (edited by Robert Ellsberg)
Oscar Romero (by Marie Dennis, Renny Golden, and Scott Wright)

Forthcoming volumes include:
Eberhard Arnold
Karl Rahner
John Main
Flannery O'Connor
Brother Roger of Taizé

MODERN SPIRITUAL MASTERS SERIES

OSCAR ROMERO

Reflections on His Life and Writings

MARIE DENNIS
RENNY GOLDEN
SCOTT WRIGHT

ORBIS BOOKS

Maryknoll, New York 10545

Sixth Printing, November 2004

The Catholic Foreign Mission Society of America (Maryknoll) recruits and trains people for overseas missionary service. Through Orbis Books, Maryknoll aims to foster the international dialogue that is essential to mission. The books published, however, reflect the opinions of their authors and are not meant to represent the official position of the society.

To obtain more information about Maryknoll and Orbis Books, please visit our website at www.maryknoll.org.

Library of Congress Cataloging-in-Publication Data

Dennis, Marie.
    Oscar Romero : reflections on his life and writings / Marie Dennis, Renny Golden, Scott Wright.
      p. cm.
    ISBN 1-57075-309-1 (pbk.)
      1. Romero, Oscar A. (Oscar Arnulfo), 1917–1980. 2. Spiritual life – Catholic Church.
    3. Christian life – Catholic authors. I. Golden, Renny. II. Wright, Scott. III. Title.
BX4705.R669 D46 2000
282′.092 – dc21
  [B]
                                            99-052262

Contents

Introduction

This is a story about an archbishop, Oscar Romero, and his people in a small country that still burns with memories of fire. In the 1980s El Salvador was a nation abandoned internationally and under the bomb and gun of a murderous army funded by the United States. Yet the tiny Central American country, with its verdant terrain, its blue volcanoes, and its malnourished children, was never, even during the worst of the violence that engulfed it, a nation far from God. On the contrary, by its faithfulness to the God of history, El Salvador became a living embodiment of its name, *el salvador,* the savior. In a world where Christianity too often has been identified with irrelevance or sentimentality, the witness of the Salvadorans and their archbishop is, for all of us in the North, salvific.

To each one of us Christ is saying, "If you want your life and mission to be fruitful like mine, do like me. Be converted into a seed that lets itself be buried. Let yourself be killed. Do not be afraid. Those who shun suffering will remain alone. No one is more alone than the selfish. But if you give your life out of love for others, as I give mine for all, you will reap a great harvest. You will have the deepest satisfactions. Do not fear death or threats. The Lord goes with you."[1]

Oscar Romero was born in Ciudad Barrios, San Miguel, in the eastern part of El Salvador on August 15, 1917, into the simple life of a rural family. His basic education was followed by an apprenticeship with a local carpenter, but his yearning to enter the seminary was ultimately realized. After studies in San Miguel and San Salvador and ordination in Rome on April 4, 1942, World War II forced Romero to abandon his doctoral studies and return to El Salvador.

His early pastoral duties included parish work, diocesan work as secretary of the San Miguel diocese, high school chaplaincy, and diocesan newspaper work. He was always considered to be a fine preacher and was careful to root his message in the daily experiences of the faithful people who listened.

In 1967 Romero accepted a new position as secretary-general of the Salvadoran Bishops Conference; soon after, he was named executive secretary of the Central American Bishops Conference and an auxiliary bishop in San Salvador. His very conservative mindset made him wary of changes in the church occasioned by the Second Vatican Council, though he was at all times a faithful son of the church. He found the thinking of the Latin American bishops gathered at Medellín in Colombia in 1968 equally troubling. The message of Medellín deliberately relocated the Latin American Catholic Church to the side of those who were poor and oppressed — especially those who suffered the impact of structural or institutional violence. The consequences were earth-shattering and difficult for those like Romero, who understood the Gospel message to be one of peace and reconciliation. The pursuit of social justice and liberation too often seemed to lead to division and conflict.

In 1971 Romero became editor of the archdiocesan newspaper, *Orientacíon*. In that position and in subsequent positions in the archdiocese, including rector of the archdiocesan seminary, he was both cautious and conservative. For years he clung to a belief in the basic goodness of those who were in power in El Salvador and was exceedingly concerned about the activities of groups who were beginning to call for an end to the social, political, and economic status quo.

In 1974 Romero was named bishop of Santiago de María in Usulután. There, official repression against the rural poor began to escalate. He was faced with an unavoidable challenge to speak out against the violence. He did so privately and politely, believing that the killings were an aberration, not government policy, and that they would be stopped once the government knew what was happening.

Romero was profoundly affected by the suffering of the poor, especially by the plight of those who worked on coffee plantations in his diocese. He opened the rectory and diocesan buildings to shelter people in need; he condemned the injustice with which they were treated. Slowly, the impoverished and violated people of his diocese led him to a better understanding of the reality they lived. Moved by compassion, he began to feel the fire of righteous anger stir in his soul and to distance himself from the powerful ones who maintained the status quo.

In February 1977, when Oscar Arnulfo Romero was installed as archbishop of San Salvador, fourteen Salvadoran families controlled over 60 percent of the arable land. The struggle for land dates to the Spanish conquest and the elite's decision in 1881 to abolish indigenous communal land rights in order to allow the coffee magnates to consolidate their holdings. The process of land theft continued until 1932, when the indigenous rose up to challenge the coffee barons' protectors, the Salvadoran military. In what Salvadorans refer to as "the Massacre," the army responded viciously. More than thirty thousand people were killed in one month. By 1961, 12 percent of the peasants were landless; by 1971, 30 percent were landless; and by 1980 an estimated 65 percent were landless.[2]

Romero came to his episcopal office a year after a minimal land reform program was initiated under an army colonel, President Arturo Armando Molina. But the large plantation owners and the extreme right wing of the army canceled the reform and targeted anyone in the rural areas who had come out in its favor. Paramilitary and military groups launched a full-scale attack on the church because of its support for peasant and workers' rights. Foreign priests were expelled from the country. Graffiti in the capital read: "Be a patriot, kill a priest."

Within weeks after Romero became archbishop, his Jesuit friend Rutilio Grande and two companions were assassinated, and Security forces opened fire at two public demonstrations in

San Salvador (February 28 in the Plaza Libertad and May 1 at Parque Cuscatlán). Within months, scores of pastoral agents and another priest, Alfonso Navarro, were killed by death squads. In 1978 and 1979 the repression intensified. Father Ernesto Barrera was killed; Father Octavio Ortiz and four young people on a retreat with him were massacred; Father Rafael Palacios and Father Alirio Napoleón Macías were assassinated. Whole villages fled into the city for refuge. Thousands of people left El Salvador for other countries.

In October 1979, a group of young reformist officers overthrew President Carlos Humberto Romero and challenged their own ruling command. They installed two different civilian governments, which eventually quit when the established military command, loyal to the oligarchy, unleashed a violent campaign of repression against any peasant, priest, or reformist officer who supported land reform. The United States later offered the Salvadoran Military High Command military and economic aid to put down the escalating insurgency if the military would support a civilian that the United States backed. Napoleón Duarte, a graduate of the University of Notre Dame, was appointed to the junta and later elected president. During the first two years of his governance, thirty thousand were killed.

Although the army insisted their war was directed at the Farabundo Martí National Liberation Front (FMLN) guerrilla opposition, they were unable to "catch" the elusive guerrillas. They then sought to cut off their "support," which the Military High Command identified as 90 percent of the population of El Salvador. Death squads were active in the rural areas, intent on cutting down peasants who organized farm cooperatives or those who supported the cause of the landless. By 1980 paramilitary and security forces escalated their counterinsurgency strategy. In January, when two hundred thousand people peacefully demonstrated in San Salvador, the military opened fire on the crowd, killing fifty and wounding scores more. To demoralize and terrify civilians into submission, the military and their accomplices not only killed but mutilated: skinning alive, slitting throats, beheading people, tearing unborn children from their mothers' wombs.

Bodies were left in village squares for the buzzards; no villager would dare touch them lest they be accused of subversion. On March 24, 1980, Archbishop Oscar Romero was brutally slain. Assassinated as he celebrated the Eucharist in the chapel of the Divine Providence hospital, he became the good shepherd who laid down his life for his flock. After Romero's death, the war in El Salvador raged on. In May 1980, refugees were massacred by the Salvadoran military as they tried to swim across the Sumpul River to reach safety in Honduras. Six hundred were killed, mostly women and children. In December 1980, four U.S. churchwomen, Maryknoll sisters Maura Clark and Ita Ford, Ursuline sister Dorothy Kazel, and Cleveland lay missioner Jean Donovan, were viciously raped and murdered. In December 1981 nearly a thousand people, again mostly women and children, were massacred by the army at El Mozote in the northern department of Morazán. At the other end of a devastating decade, in November 1989, six Jesuit priests and two women who worked with them were slaughtered.

Throughout those years the violence was absolutely unrelenting. In each of these cases, the violence was carried out by a military funded by the United States and by officers and soldiers trained at the U.S. Army School of the Americas.

Romero, simply by being a pastor, tried to prevent this war that was being waged against the poor. He gave the people hope against all human logic, calling upon their deep reserves of faith in God and defending their right to organize for justice. In his weekly homilies, which were broadcast by radio, he named the massacres and tortures, unmasking the hideousness of a war directed against civilians. He confronted the disinformation apparatus of low-intensity conflict by refusing to allow right-wing sectors in the United States or in El Salvador to characterize either the Salvadoran people or himself as subversives.

No other Salvadoran carried the moral authority to subvert the strategies of low-intensity counterinsurgency warfare. Romero's nonviolent prophetic stance effectively compromised the government's primary objective — winning the hearts and minds of the people.

Oscar Romero, the shy pastor, became, for the sake of those who were defenseless, a public bishop whose spirituality was not hidden. He lived in the open space of history, and he died there, lifting his voice for the voiceless. The essence of his spirituality is that he found in the poor a prophetic voice that neither a sniper's bullet nor his own timidity could muffle.

We must save not the soul at the hour of death but the person living in history.[3]

Romero was a traditional cleric, a conservative theologian, a generous but reserved pastor, a man given to regular solitary times of prayer. Though a person of scrupulous self-criticism and asceticism, he discovered a God who was enmeshed in the ordinary, messy, conflictive struggle of the Salvadoran people. For Romero, the people were a source of grace. Although his love for the poor would cost him his life, he was not a tragic figure but one who seemed remarkably grateful for the gift of his people's love. Thus he was "pulled" forward into a holiness which he had not anticipated but which he discovered in the people's call and the demands of history.

As Romero surrendered to the demands of the Gospel, he gave voice to a church of the poor and embraced a belief in the historical dimension of liberation even as he held tightly to the transcendent dimension as well. When his fellow bishops accused him of staining the church with politics, he never retaliated. Over and over he proclaimed his desire that all be converted to the God of life who was revealed most fully among the defiled, the downtrodden, the outcasts.

By choosing the poor, Romero did not intend to cut off the rich, the government, or the military. On the contrary, he called them to conversion. When the powerful turned against him, he called for their conversion. When the security forces plotted his murder, he embraced them with love. Like his mentor Jesus, he called for forgiveness in the midst of his people's crucifixion.

Therefore, dear brothers and sisters, especially those of you who hate me, who think I am preaching violence, who de-

fame me and know it isn't true, you that have hands stained with murder, with torture, with atrocity, with injustice — be converted. I love you deeply. I am sorry for you because you go on the way to ruin.[4]

I ask the faithful people who listen to me with love and devotion to pardon me for saying this, but it gives me more pleasure that my enemies listen to me. I know that the reason they listen to me is that I bear them a message of love. I don't hate them. I don't want revenge. I wish them no harm. I beg them to be converted, to come to be happy with the happiness that you faithful ones have.[5]

Romero preached that the poor were the good news of God, that the poor — not the magisterium, the episcopacy, or theologians — were the source of holiness.

Romero's life was characterized by qualities common to exemplary or saintly lives throughout history: fidelity to God; surrender of one's own self, whether unto death or in a lifetime commitment to justice, peace, and love; forgiveness of one's enemies; and a willingness to follow God beyond the demarcated path, peacefully enduring the often calumnious judgment by church and by state that such authenticity demands. Romero embodied these classical categories of holiness. He also broke them open and revealed their meaning in a new way.

Romero's spirituality — his life, his prophetic clarity, even his confusion — reminds us that spirituality is less an effort than a gift, less an individual accomplishment than a discovery of grace in our personal and social lives, less a seeking of "saints" than an unfolding of our own vulnerability and authenticity where the mystery of God pulls us forward. St. Paul's identification of love as the greatest of virtues makes holiness relational and historical. Holiness is not cultivated alone but in community. We don't learn to become saints the way concert pianists or ballerinas discipline themselves to virtuosity. Holiness is a commitment and a grace, something we seek, but mostly a gift — for Romero, a gift of God and the poor whom he loved.

Romero was great-hearted because he allowed the poor to change his heart. That was his message — that the poor are a sacrament who can transform our lives if we are willing to open ourselves to them, to accompany them.

Oscar Romero believed in the ability of subjugated people to know the truth about social reality, and he trusted their imaginative capacity to create an alternative path. Never just a theorist, he took part in the people's journey. Romero's importance comes from the fact that his prophetic voice addressed the effects of policies that leave the poor behind. Confronted with death on the streets each morning, the Salvadorans spoke not of darkness, but of slivers of light that illumined small "openings." Romero's life is an opening that allows us to question power and to find hope rather than despair among the poor of our world who struggle for dignity in spite of structures and policies that continue to oppress them.

Romero's great act of faith was that he believed in the poor. He saw them as protagonists, organizers in forging their own destinies and rebuilding their shattered communities. He was willing to bet his life on this conviction. He was willing to risk his ecclesial reputation, to be considered a dupe of the popular organizations, a puppet of the progressive Jesuits. It was inconceivable to the powerful of the church and the state that the peasants and common laborers could hold so much attraction for him. They simply could not see what he saw. He saw their dignity, their sense of humor in spite of the horror, their ingenuity when all doors of protection had closed on them. He saw their agony and their hope — in a word, he saw the face of God.

In all the years of seminary training, years in Rome, years of prayer, he had never walked with God as he did now in poor country villages. He had never been touched by God until he was touched by the hands of a mother who came to the Archdiocesan Legal Aid Office, Socorro Jurídico, only to find that her son's mutilated body had been eaten by dogs. Romero had taken as his own the heart of the poor.

One begins to experience faith and conversion when one has the heart of the poor, when one knows that financial capital, political influence, and power are worthless, and that without God we are nothing.[6]

Romero is a twentieth-century prophet whose life is not only a symbol but a gift to those of us who struggle as we search for a spiritual path for the new millennium. He often said that we run the risk of becoming insensitive to suffering and death. In all of his homilies, he tried to make the world see the value of every human life and feel the pain behind each death. Five days before his death, he spoke to a group of foreign journalists about the important role that they played:

You are the ones who bring the photograph of our people to the world.... Help them understand our situation so that they might offer us their solidarity.... Don't forget that we are people, and we are dying, fleeing, and taking refuge in the mountains.[7]

Don't forget.... This is the task before us. Why is it so important not to forget the suffering of the Salvadoran people? Or any people? What does it mean to remember the stories of countless poor and humble Salvadoran families who were dying, fleeing, and taking refuge in the mountains for more than a decade of war that eventually cost the lives of seventy-five thousand people and profoundly touched the lives of five million more? These are questions we address. And there are always more questions than there are answers when we reflect on the mystery of faith and God's grace, as well as on the mystery of betrayal and evil.

Today the situation in El Salvador is still grim after twelve years of war, seventy-five thousand deaths, and fragile peace accords. After so much bloodshed, one out of four Salvadoran children still dies of a curable illness before the age of five and the average family still makes only $400 a year. As in the past, the poor are aware that they are impoverished victims of economic structures and systems that oppress and exclude them and against which they rebel.

Yet they are the heirs of a legacy of a remarkable, even miraculous humanity that faced the ballast of an inferno and clung to each other and to the God of life. The base Christian communities understand themselves not simply as the recipients of the Gospel, but as proclaimers of good news, of light and salvation to the world. The story of Oscar Romero and his people is good news for us, too.

Goodness persists: in the spunky, irrepressible passion of the Salvadorans who were able to resist the architects of a brutal war and struggle, and in the memories of those who gave their lives for the cause of the poor, especially in the memory of their fallen pastor who gave his life for his people and in so doing left all of us a legacy of hope.

The poor were Romero's Magnificat. They were the psalm that he prayed. His prophetic imagination and compassionate heart are revealed through his interaction with a people in whom he found God. His was a theology, a spirituality, developed on the move, in the crucible of suffering and hope, that can perhaps be discerned only through reflection on the historical context in which his spirituality was molded.

We can also, of course, discern Romero's spirituality by taking him at his word. He was a preacher and a theologian. His word is preserved in the pastoral letters he wrote to the church of El Salvador, in carefully documented homilies, in his diary and letters, and in public talks such as "The Political Dimension of the Christian Faith," which he gave at the University of Louvain in Belgium. He wrote these in his small room late into the night after long days of responding as a pastor to conflict and brutality, massacres, church takeovers, encounters with mothers whose children had been killed, and endless meetings.

I am going to speak to you simply as a pastor, as one who, together with his people, has been learning the beautiful but harsh truth that the Christian faith does not cut us off from the world but immerses us in it, that the church is not a fortress set apart from the city. The church follows Jesus who lived, worked, struggled and died in the midst of a city, in the polis. It is in this sense that I should like to talk about the political dimension of the Christian faith: in the precise sense of the repercussions of faith on the world and also of the repercussions that being in the world has on faith.[8]

1

The Centrality of the Poor

In his brief three years as archbishop, Romero was eminently a pastor, constantly moving closer to his people in their impoverished rural communities and marginal urban parishes. But he was also a prophet, and in the end he was a martyr, mixing his own blood with the blood of his people. In each of these ways — as pastor, prophet, and martyr — Oscar Romero united the love of God and the love of the poor with the heart of a mystic.

> *We learn to see the face of Christ — the face of Christ that also is the face of a suffering human being, the face of the crucified, the face of the poor, the face of a saint, and the face of every person — and we love each one with the criteria with which we will be judged: "I was hungry and you gave me to eat."*[1]

Saints are defined as prophets, martyrs, mystics, or healers. Some cross over these categories. But rarely is a prophet at the same time also a mystic, or vice versa. Prophetic types who are caught in the fire of history and nudged by the great maw of justice rarely court the inner realms of mysticism. Conversely, mystics are said to avoid the marketplace and to seek the gates of silence which swing open to the rapture of God.

But these categories suggest an inaccurate dualism. Few prophets could endure the scandal and scourge they evoke without an inner life of fathomless depth and intensity. And few who climb the mystical mountain of Carmel reach the great heights of Mystery without walking back down to embrace the rag-tag people pushing history toward blessing or curse.

The challenge for any contemporary spirituality is: "How do we speak of God in the midst of unjust suffering?" Such a spirituality would have to combine in a unique way, as Oscar Romero's did, both the prophetic and contemplative dimensions of spirituality. Mystical language expresses the gratuitousness of God's love; prophetic language expresses the demands this love makes. As Gustavo Gutiérrez writes,

> Without the prophetic dimension the language of contemplation is in danger of having no grip on the history in which God acts and in which we meet God. Without the mystical dimension the language of prophecy can narrow its vision and weaken its perception of God who makes all things new.... Both languages arise, among the poor of Latin America as in Job, out of the suffering and hopes of the innocent.[2]

In a very real sense, Romero's spirituality is the *spirit of the poor.* Romero found the poor of El Salvador to be truly blessed with spirit. As he opened his heart to them, they in turn gave back a hundredfold.

The spirituality of Oscar Romero is *a Gospel spirit* imbued with the paschal mystery of death and resurrection. Like Jesus, in his words, deeds, and witness, Romero communicated to the poor as no other the good news that God loves them in a special way.

The spirituality of Oscar Romero is also a *spirit made flesh in the crucible of Salvadoran history,* a spirit of life in conflict with the idols of death. Romero's story is one with the story of a people struggling to break free from the bondage of oppression, wandering in the wilderness of social exclusion for years, and yearning to reach that Promised Land of justice and peace. His words attest to the demands of that journey:

> *Either we serve the life of Salvadorans or we are accomplices in their death.*[3]

The spirituality of Oscar Romero is, finally, *a spirit of the martyrs*. To be a martyr in El Salvador is to share fully in the fate of the poor. In Romero's words,

> *The greatest sign of faith in a God of life is the witness of those who are willing to give up their own life.*[4]

Romero's accompaniment of his people was an accompaniment to the grave and to glory.

Accompaniment of the poor, the Gospel, history, and martyrdom: these were defined by Romero as the marks of a church of the poor. They are the signs of Romero's spirituality as well. Drawing near to the poor, he became poor. Proclaiming the Gospel as good news to the poor, he became that good news. Protecting the life of the poor against the powers of death in history, his life became a defense of the poor. Commemorating the martyrdom of his people, he, too, became a martyr. In the end, Oscar Romero gave life to the poor as a light to the world. True to the ancient wisdom of the church, his martyr's blood has become the seed of new life:

> *Frequently I have been threatened with death. I should tell you that, as a Christian, I don't believe in death without resurrection. If they kill me, I will be resurrected in the Salvadoran people.*[5]

Some prophets are mystics. Some are prophets, mystics, and martyrs. Oscar Arnulfo Romero was one of these. Whatever Rome's canonization decision, the people of Latin America have declared him their great saint.

The spirituality of Archbishop Oscar Romero cannot be understood apart from the Salvadoran people, especially the poor majority whom he loved. During the war years the term *entregado* referred to someone who completely gave himself or herself to the people. Archbishop Oscar Romero was *entregado*. Romero's entry into the world of the poor brought him face to face with his people, crucified by poverty and tortured by violence. There Romero discovered, in the wounds of the poor, a source of life, light, and salvation for the world.

With this people it is not hard to be a good shepherd. They are a people that impel to their service us who have been called to defend their rights and to be their voice.[6]

We have begun, then, by entering into the dramatic history of Oscar Romero's people, where the lives of the poor in El Salvador were — and still are — at risk, and death comes to the poor before their time. The history of the people's struggle for liberation is the fertile soil in which the seed of Romero's spirituality took root and bore fruit. We must know something of their passion and death before we can know anything of their resurrection and the spirit of new life.

Monseñor, as the people called him, is considered the great saint of the Americas because his life so deeply revealed an unequivocal faithfulness to the impoverished and the despised. Few clerics in recent memory have articulated in word and deed such a profound love of the poor. Few bishops have so *publicly* defended their people against a totalitarian state, much less one that was tacitly supported by the majority of the Salvadoran bishops and directed by the United States government.

Remarkably, the hour of the inferno was also the hour of resistance to the flames of hate. When violence against civilians — and against the church and its pastoral workers — mounted daily, the Salvadorans spoke, not of obliteration, not of the doors of safety that slammed shut, but of the "openings." This charism of the Salvadorans to imagine the possible even as the army sealed off escape, reflects and replicates, perhaps inspired, Romero's own imaginative capacity. These were Romero's sentiments at the height of terror:

Let us not be afraid brothers and sisters. We are living through difficult and uncertain days. We do not know if this very evening we will be prisoners or murder victims.... But one thing I do know: even those who have disappeared after arrest, even those who are mourned in the mystery of an abduction, are known and loved by God.... He loves us.... He loves our history, too.[7]

In early 1980, when corpses were piled high daily in the public garbage dumps outside San Salvador, when bishops, nuncios, and government officials demanded neutrality, Oscar Romero chose the side of the outcasts, standing virtually alone in his defense of the "nobodies" of history. The poor, he believed, were the place of God's revelation in history. They were the "opening" where Romero saw light pouring into the eclipsing rise of violence. They were the opening where the God of hope and possibility was discovered in the midst of blood and dismemberment. They were *what mattered:*

> *Let us not measure the church by the number of its members or by its material buildings. . . . Many buildings have been stolen from her and turned into libraries and barracks, and markets. It doesn't matter. The material walls here will be left behind in history. What matters is you, the people, your hearts.*[8]

In choosing the side of the poor majority, Romero was perceived to have indicted, and then written off, the powerful. This was never his intention. On the contrary, he invited the powerful over and over again to be converted to the God of justice and compassion. But neutrality in the face of such mass persecution, he said, was impossible.

> *You have to understand that the conflict is between the government and the people. There is conflict with the church because we take the people's side. I insist that the church is not looking for a fight with the government, and for my part I do not want disputes with the government. When they tell me I am a subversive and that I meddle in political matters, I say it's not true. I try to define the church's mission, which is a prolongation of Christ's. The church must save the people and be with them in their search for justice. Also, it must not let them follow ways of hatred, vengeance, or unjust violence. In this sense, we accompany the people, a people that suffers greatly. Of course, those that trample the people must be in conflict with the church.*[9]

Romero was a "saint" who defended the disposable ones, the impoverished castoffs left on the killing floors of a postmodern world. He did not die in peace, acclaimed by the church and the state. He died a violent death that would challenge the fidelity of the church and the power of the state. Romero, who had spent years embracing a traditional, disincarnate theology, chose, for the sake of the Gospel, to enter the arena of secular power. Defense of the poor required him to engage the structural forces that produced their poverty. What was once said by Dom Helder Camara could have been said by Romero: "When I advocated feeding the hungry, they called me a saint; but when I asked why they were poor, they called me a Communist."

What would lead a conservative, Rome-educated cleric to be suspected of Communist leanings and a quiet, reserved son of humble parents to be proclaimed the great saint of the Americas?

In February 1977, two Salvadorans named Romero were elected to the most powerful offices of church and state within days of each other. On February 26 the minister of defense, General Carlos Humberto Romero, was finally declared president after a week of protests against a fraudulent election. Days before, on February 22, Oscar Arnulfo Romero, a moderate conservative ecclesiastic, was installed as the archbishop of San Salvador. No one protested his election except the organized poor who feared the new archbishop would reverse the progressive direction of his predecessor, Archbishop Luis Chávez y González.

> I worked with various progressive priests in the peasant organization. We were in a meeting when the news arrived about the naming of Romero. Without saying so, all had feared that this would happen. And it did. We felt it was a huge victory for the conservative oligarchy. And we prepared to confront him. (Nidia Díaz)[10]

Shortly before his installation, Oscar Romero wrote to his priests calling them to ecclesial fraternity and transcendent witness. Nothing he said gave any indication he would challenge anything. His installation was a great relief to the powerful, tired of the aging Archbishop Chávez who couldn't control his clergy. It was a relief also for the other Salvadoran bishops, who feared the appointment of Bishop Arturo Rivera y Damas, a supporter of Chávez's who endorsed "the option for the poor" espoused by the Latin American bishops at the watershed ecclesial conference at Medellín, Colombia, in 1968. Romero was safe. He could be trusted to counter leftist priests and nuns. In spite of the fact that Romero had attended the Medellín conference taking copious notes, he distrusted practitioners of the new liberation theology. Seven months before his election Romero preached against revolutionary, "hate-filled christologies." Recalling the dread felt when he was elected, Jesuit theologian Jon Sobrino observed, "We all thought we faced a very bleak future."[11]

Oscar Arnulfo Romero had been a pious boy, a holy priest, and dedicated auxiliary bishop. He was well respected by the Salvadoran military, government officials, and the best families in his small country. His quiet intelligence and strict theological orthodoxy were appreciated by his fellow Salvadoran bishops, the nuncio, and the Roman curia.

Conversely, his election as the archbishop of San Salvador was received by the Salvadoran people as one more blow to the collective body of an impoverished, colonized people.

Within three weeks of his installation as archbishop, extraordinary events would alter the course of Salvadoran history and the lives of both Romeros. Wealthy landowners were well rid of Archbishop Chávez's support for landless peasants, but they still considered the church a threat and had increased pressure on the president to act decisively on their behalf. The government responded by increasing persecution of the church.

Warnings were clear. Five foreign priests were deported; but the next strike would be at the heart of the Salvadoran church. A priest would be murdered. The target was Salvadoran Jesuit Rutilio Grande, who worked with a team of seminarians and catechists building base Christian communities in Aguilares, a rural area that was part of the archdiocese of San Salvador.

Grande had publicly denounced rich landowners who held virtually all the fertile land, crowding peasants to the rocky sides of mountains. In a nation where fourteen families owned 60 percent of the arable land, to defend the peasant farmer's right to land was a deeply courageous act. This was particularly true because the fourteen families were backed by the National Guard, the National Police, the Treasury Police, the Salvadoran military, a corrupt judicial system, and a president and Legislative Assembly who dared not countermand this monolithic rule.

Rutilio Grande had anointed too many half-starved infants who had died from dysentery or malnutrition. He continued to speak out against misery, despite the costs.

A plan to kill a priest, however, was unprecedented. Whether President Molina was aware of the plan is not clear. That the president-elect, Carlos Humberto Romero, was aware, if not implicated, is likely.

On March 12, Rutilio Grande was traveling in a jeep with an old man and a boy through the tall sugarcane fields toward El Paisnal to celebrate an evening Mass. Halfway between Aguilares and El Paisnal, marksmen, lying in wait, opened fire and killed all three.

Informed of Grande's assassination, Romero called still-acting President Molina to demand an investigation. Then he left for Aguilares, arriving at 10 pm. By the time Romero offered a Mass for the three and left at midnight, something had transformed him. A peasant pastoral worker describes that night of grief and the surprise of Romero's response:

I took off [Rutilio Grande's] socks, all soaked in blood. I helped prepare his body for burial. When I heard the news, I felt as if I was being lifted up into the air and then suddenly dropped to the ground. I was so bewildered I don't even know how I got to the church. And now I wonder how I was able to get through everything that happened that day. I loved him. That's why I kept a small piece of cloth with his blood on it.

The priests gave me permission to be there for the two nights of the wake in the church at Aguilares. Together we all recalled the wonderful communities we had formed with him.

It was midnight when Monseñor arrived to view Father Grande's body. He went up to the table where we had placed him, wrapped in a white sheet, and stood there looking at him, and the way he looked at him you could tell how much he loved him too. Until that moment we didn't really know Monseñor. And that night for the first time we heard his voice in his homily.

As we listened to him we were very surprised. "He has the same voice as Father Grande!" we all said. Because it seemed that at that moment the voice of Father Rutilio passed to Monseñor. Right then and there. Really.

"Could it be," I whispered to my friend, "that God has worked this miracle for us so that we would not be left orphans?" (Ernestina Rivera)[12]

While it is impossible to know the heart of another or to understand the depth of spiritual conversion that prepared Romero for such an event, those who knew him unanimously agree that after Rutilio Grande's murder, Oscar Romero was never the same.

There is little doubt that the assassination of a good priest and a good friend profoundly affected Romero. He had chosen this country pastor to be the master of ceremonies for his elevation to archbishop only a month before. Father Grande had been prefect of discipline at the seminary when Romero was living there with the Jesuits. Rutilio was an exemplary priest: humble, serious, prayerful.

Romero, however, was concerned about Grande's pastoral direction in Aguilares. It was too radical, too much in line with the Medellín process of evangelization that he considered dangerous, subject to manipulation and confrontation. In a word, it was too political. Yet the experience of viewing Grande's body impacted him deeply. Salvadoran Jesuit Jon Sobrino says that as

Romero "stood gazing at the mortal remains of Rutilio Grande,
the scales fell from his eyes."[13] The scales were fear of anything
that might "immerse the church in the ambiguous, conflictive
flesh of history."[14] For Sobrino the moment was decisive:

> I believe that the murder of Rutilio Grande was the occasion
> of the conversion of Archbishop Romero. . . . It was Rutilio's
> death that gave Archbishop Romero the strength for new
> activity . . . and the fundamental direction for his own life.[15]

Yet Romero himself never spoke of his conversion, although
he would continually exhort Salvadorans to be converted to the
side of the poor:

> *The poor person is the one who has been converted to God
> and puts all his faith in him, and the rich person is one who
> has not been converted to God and puts his confidence in
> idols: money, power, material things. . . . Our work should
> be directed toward converting ourselves and all people to
> this authentic meaning of poverty.*[16]

Perhaps Romero, the son of humble parents, felt his love of
the poor was undeviating. Perhaps he could not "see," as could
those around him, the radical change that followed that fateful
night. Romero does not tell us explicitly about his conversion to
the people, but the poor understood it very well.

Care for the poor had been consistent in his life as auxiliary
bishop of Santiago de María, and perhaps some seeds of radical change were planted there as he realized the injustice suffered
by coffee workers in his diocese. But choosing their side, facing
the forces aligned against them, entering the conflictive, messy
path of history — that was another matter. However devastated
Romero was to encounter the body of the martyred priest, the
transformation that would claim him was not due only to Rutilio Grande's death. What accounts for his magnificent "about
face" was the same claim that drew Rutilio to risk his life: the
Salvadoran poor.

Imagine the scene that night. The church is packed. Peasants
who can't enter the overflowing church stand outside. There is

not a sound as the archbishop walks up the aisle to the spot where the three bodies lie beneath white sheets before the altar. After Romero prays he turns to begin Mass, and he looks out at the faces of the poor. Hundreds of peasants stare back at him. They say nothing. Their silence interrogates Romero. The peasants' eyes ask the question he alone can answer: Will you stand with us as Rutilio did?

A "hundred years of solitude" gathered a voice, the voice without a voice. Romero's yes was not spoken in words. He would answer with deeds. In the end, he would give all he had to give. Yes, until death silenced him.

> *I want to . . . ask for your prayers that I be faithful to this promise, that I will not abandon my people. Rather, I will run with them all the risks that my ministry demands.*[17]

He never looked back. The peasants had asked for a good shepherd, and that night they got one. They, in turn would never abandon him. It is a promise the poor never broke.

That night Oscar Romero understood that the peasants of Aguilares were the church of God. This, it seems, is how the "scales fell from his eyes": he recognized God in the poor. The passion they were enduring was Christ's suffering in history. Among them, walking with them, he would fulfill his childhood longing to follow the path of Christ.

Discovering that the church is much more than the hierarchy, Rome, theologians, or clerics — more than the institution — that the church is the people, was certainly a teaching he was familiar with from Vatican II and Medellín. But that night he *experienced* God present in the people. Romero understood the poor as a sacrament of salvation. *"God needs the people themselves,"* he said, *"to save the world."*[18]

In the following months and years more priests would be killed in El Salvador, and thousands of humble Salvadorans murdered. Each death was a tragedy and a moment of grace that drew forth from him greater courage and confidence. With each murder, the very church that the powerful of El Salvador wanted to obliterate bloomed. The church of the poor grew like a field of wildflowers that shoot up the next season after the scythes have felled them, thicker and more lush than before. It was not the defense of slain priests that drove Romero. It was proclaiming the kingdom of God revealed among the inauspicious, the forgotten, the disposable poor. That was the revelation he received on the night of Grande's assassination. The church existed to serve the poor, not the other way around.

> *The church principally exists for the evangelization of the human race. Yes, it is an institution; it is made up of persons, and it has forms and structures. But all of this is for a more basic reality: the exercise of its task of evangelization.*[19]

> *This ideal brings together all the dimensions of human reality, excluding none, and it does not reduce the faith merely to the improvements of the social or political order. Today, however, we should stress the social and historical dimensions of this liberation, as Puebla requested: "Confronted with the realities that are part of our lives today, we must learn from the Gospel that in Latin America we cannot truly love our fellow human beings, and hence God, unless we commit ourselves on the personal level and, in many cases, on the structural level as well, to serving and promoting the most dispossessed and downtrodden human groups and social classes, with all the consequences that will entail on the plane of temporal realities." The church, then, would betray its own love for God and its fidelity to the Gospel if it stopped being the "voice for the voiceless," a defender of the rights of the poor, a promoter of every just aspiration for liberation, a guide, an empowerer, a humanizer of every legitimate struggle to achieve a more just society, a society that prepares the way for the true kingdom of God in history.*[20]

This revelation accounts for Romero's conversion. Who else but God could be the source of such a change? How could a fifty-nine-year-old ecclesiastic at the pinnacle of church power, a

man of circumspection, diplomacy, filial obedience, and orthodoxy, who enjoyed the esteem of Rome and his brother bishops,
a man well received by the Salvadoran elite — how could such
a man turn away from what seemed to be a well-established life
path? Only, it seems, by invitation of a God he had long before
decided to follow, no matter what the cost.

Such a transformation was not completed that night, but it
was begun. The next day Archbishop Romero would make a decision that would put church and state on notice. In an all-day
consultation with the clergy of the archdiocese it was decided
that they would bring Rutilio Grande's body to San Salvador and
Romero would concelebrate a commemorative Mass in the plaza
outside the cathedral.

In addition, Romero made the exceptional decision to cancel
all other Masses in the archdiocese the following Sunday. He invited all the faithful to celebrate a single Mass in the cathedral of
San Salvador.

> Those opposed to the single Mass argued that it would be
> misunderstood and many would complain at not being able
> to get to Mass and Holy Communion; it could also seem
> like a pure show of power. Those in favor argued that the
> Mass should be linked to the reality of life, that the single
> Mass would show in a pastoral way the exceptional condi-
> tions in the country, that it could be a good catechesis on the
> Mass itself, and that the lack of other Masses would show
> what expulsions of priests from the country could lead to.[21]

At the Mass, he made public his support for all priests who
were in danger of persecution: *"Whoever touches one of my
priests, touches me."* There he received the public acclamation of
the people who, in a gesture that would become the hallmark of
his Sunday homilies in the cathedral, enthusiastically applauded
his words:

> *Thank you. This applause ratifies the profound joy I feel
> in my heart in taking possession of the archdiocese: just to*

know that my weaknesses, my inabilities find their comple-
ment, their strength, their courage in a unified priesthood.[22]

A single Sunday Mass in all of the archdiocese was provocative
enough, but there was more. All Catholic schools would close for
three days. Finally, and this can only be described as the act of
a man with a soul on fire, Romero refused to meet with the Salvadoran government until the repression ceased. As archbishop
he never attended an official event. A timid man had "overnight"
become a prophet.

As Romero said during Rutilio Grande's funeral Mass in
Aguilares, *"This is not the moment to speak about my per-*
sonal relationship with Father Grande, but rather to gather
from this cadaver a message for all of us who continue the pil-
grimage." And he would add, *"Let us not forget. We are a*
pilgrim church, exposed to misunderstanding, to persecution; but
a church that walks peacefully because we carry within us the
force of love."[23]

Romero did not simply give voice to the voiceless poor by act-
ing as their prophetic advocate. Like Rutilio Grande, he trusted
their voice and their ability to make decisions that affected their
fate and thus the fate of the church. And he trusted his own cler-
ical community and diocesan pastoral workers to do the same.
Two dynamics characterized Romero's decisions: collaboration
and a democratic process. In the eight hours of meetings held
to decide the church's response to the murders of Rutilio Grande
and his companions, Romero sat silently through rounds of small
group discussions and a series of votes until there was suffi-
cient agreement to move forward. From the beginning Romero
solicited his pastoral workers' and clergy's help in "reading the
signs of the times" and developing appropriate pastoral strategies
in response.

This trust in the people was not only a sign of his humility; it
was a cornerstone of his pastoral ministry. And it was a characteristic that dramatically diverged from the hierarchical practices
of the Catholic Church. In fact, from this and similar practices an
esteem grew among both the people and the clergy that rankled

his fellow bishops, who maintained their ties to the government and oligarchy. Like a popular teacher he was accused of "playing to the crowd," of relishing the attention he was given. He examined his conscience about this in his diary, and, though a self-critical person, concluded that the people's love for him and his for them was untainted. In a simple and self-possessed assertion he concluded that the problem was not his, but the bishops'.

> *I went to have dinner with the secretary of the Cursillos de Cristiandad. It was a family dinner, and I introduced a topic that was explored in a very Christian and evangelical way: the theme of unity; asking them to suggest to me in a fraternal way what I can do to achieve unity with my dear brother bishops. Because if I am the cause of any obstacle to this unity, then I am willing to fix that.... They told me that unity must involve the criterion expressed in the Gospels; that unity is one of the fruits of the Holy Spirit and that the people many times interpret this Spirit better than the hierarchy itself does; and that, according to this evangelical criteria and the Holy Spirit, there was no doubt that the course we have adopted in the archdiocese is the work of God.*[24]

Romero understood immediately that prophetic action would put him in harm's way: *"This is the risk of any prophetic mission of the church, to be criticized even by your own people and to find yourself alone."*[25] What he had not fully anticipated was the way in which the other bishops and papal nuncio would turn against him. Immediately after he issued the bulletin announcing the single Sunday Mass and declaring that he would not participate in official government affairs until the repression ended, the papal nuncio, Archbishop Gerada, sent for him. He told him the single Mass was provocative and dangerous, that his actions were "irresponsible, imprudent, and inconsistent."[26] Romero refused to budge. The Mass, he quietly informed the nuncio, would take place.

In spite of his decision, he sought unity with his brother bishops. After he appealed to them for support, to no avail, he decided to poll once again the Salvadoran clergy. He called a meeting that gathered over seventy clerics, the majority of whom were pastors. He wanted one more assessment of their willingness to support or challenge the single Mass.

He had already confronted his own scruple about the single Mass. It was a preoccupation that revealed the traditionalist that he was: *"If the Eucharist gives glory to God,"* Romero asked, *"will not God have more glory in the usual number of Sunday Masses than in just one?"*[27]

Jon Sobrino was astounded: "I must confess my heart sank to hear him. Here was a theology straight out of the dark ages."[28]

Romero's prophetic theology, which sought to defend the poor, was strong, clear, and uncompromising, but his "personal" spirituality was fastened to a more conservative tradition, discipline, and language. What worried Romero was rarely the danger he faced in standing for the people and against the government. Once he felt the path of love was clear he walked forward without hesitation. Perplexity arose if he feared imprudence, that he might endanger others, or that he failed to give glory to God. At times his spirituality scrambled to catch up with his theology. At other times it seemed the reverse — that spiritually Romero had chosen the path of the God of history, but he still had to articulate his theology "on the road" as he walked.

Deeper, perhaps, than any of the visible changes that Romero made was the inner journey that must have taken place in his heart. Sobrino believes that what was at stake in his decision to have only one Mass was his understanding of God. Only when Jesuit provincial César Jerez convinced Romero that the church father Irenaeus defined "God's glory" as the "living person" could Romero act with confidence.

The people, and preeminently the poor, reveal the glory of God; their struggle for liberation from suffering and sinful structures that oppress them locates the reign of God in the human story. This was the essence of Romero's theology. And his Christology flowed from this understanding. In the face of the poor he saw the face of Christ crucified:

> *Each time we look upon the poor, on the farmworkers who harvest the coffee, the sugarcane, or the cotton, or the farmer who joins the caravan of workers looking to earn their savings for the year...remember, there is the face of Christ....*
>
> *The face of Christ is among the sacks and baskets of the farmworker; the face of Christ is among those who are tortured and mistreated in the prisons; the face of Christ is dying of hunger in the children who have nothing to eat; the face of Christ is in the poor who ask the church for their voice to be heard. How can the church deny this request when it is Christ who is telling us to speak for him?*[29]

A traditionalist, Romero was willing to interrogate his most deeply held theological beliefs for the sake of the poor who became, for him, a gospel. And that is what he preached:

> *A church that tries to keep itself pure and uncontaminated would not be a church of God's service to people. The authentic church is one that does not mind conversing with prostitutes and publicans and sinners, as Christ did — and with Marxists and those of various political movements — in order to bring them salvation's true message.*[30]

He was determined also to act in communion with those he believed defended the poor. The decision to have a single Mass and to close the schools evolved through dialogue. A man who had spent his adult life brokering and embracing the protocols of ecclesiastical power called for democracy as the fundamental process of community building. When the seventy clerics voted a second time, all but one affirmed the single Mass. Romero was assured. Though he would face Goliath, he would do so as a representative of the church of the Salvadoran people, faithful to the Gospel; his weapon, that of the weak throughout history — a Gospel that defended the victim and questioned the powerful.

Almost two and a half years later, when another priest, Rafael Palacios, was assassinated, Romero would articulate the fruit of communal reflection that began so early in his episcopal tenure:

I interpreted this single Mass as a gesture of solidarity on the part of the archdiocese for three purposes: first, to reaffirm the infinite and divine value of the Eucharist, which is profaned by excessive individualism and celebrations held for reasons that are not always consistent with the divine will. Second, we are also expressing our appreciation for the priesthood, specifically in memory of a dead priest, vilely assassinated, and showing what the church is like when it is empty of the Eucharist and of priests as were all the churches of the diocese on this day of one single Mass. And in the third place, to show the united voice of the people of God, a people who prays, a people who protests the attacks that have been made against it, but does not do this out of hatred or a desire for vengeance, but as a people who calls for sinners to be converted.[31]

After the death of Rutilio Grande, Romero would use his position to defend the tortured, the murdered, the imprisoned and terrorized masses. His Sunday homilies, which were broadcast throughout the nation, would become an island of hope in a sea of blood. Photojournalist Jim Harney reflected on the experience of hearing Romero speak:

When Romero entered the cathedral and walked down the aisle, he was followed by applause. It was as if he himself was the word of hope even before he spoke. And then when he spoke...leading up to the point when he would list the deaths and assassinations of the week, the clapping would swell to a crescendo. From the response of the people, he seemed to gain power. It was not the cadenced contrapuntal preaching of a Martin Luther King...but it was like that, insofar as the audience became part of the homily's force and imagination. He occasionally looked down at his prepared words, but mostly he spoke freely from the heart. It was incredible to see the people's response to him.[32]

His conversion to the struggle of the people for justice, whose cross revealed the dying and resurrected God of history, became one of the critical markers of his spirituality. Its essence was shaped by his growing capacity to throw in his lot with the vulnerable.

At Puebla we declared, "The situation of inhuman poverty in which millions of Latin Americans live is the most devastating and humiliating kind of scourge. And this situation finds expression in such things as a high rate of infant mortality, lack of adequate housing, health problems, starvation wages, unemployment and underemployment, malnutrition, job uncertainty, compulsory mass migrations, etc." Experiencing these realities and letting ourselves be affected by them, far from separating us from our faith, has sent us back to the world of the poor as to our true home.[33]

The poor were alone, as Romero was often alone. Yet they had each other. It was never enough to denounce rape, electric shock treatment, beheadings, torture, and the deaths of tens of thousands of people. Yet in the torture chambers of clandestine jails, in Mariona and Ilopango prison, Romero's words were scrawled, scratched, and recited. Most of all his words were repeated and remembered, if only silently. His words were a blessing that made sense of the madness.

As Romero discovered the crucified in the swollen bodies left in the streets and roads and garbage dumps, as he looked into the terrified eyes of mothers who came to the archdiocesan offices seeking information about disappeared spouses or children, as he blessed the broken bodies of priests who had stood with their parishioners, he embraced the Christ of history. He spoke against the wielders of violent repression and he spoke to those who suffered, to those who resisted, to those who succumbed. This was his prophetic gift — not simply to have spoken truth to power — but to have called the journey through death "salvific" and full of hope:

> *God and human beings make history. God saves humanity in the history of one's own people. The history of salvation will be El Salvador's history when we Salvadorans seek in our history the presence of God the Savior.*[34]

Romero proclaimed the Word in such a way that it became flesh in the conflictual history of El Salvador and gave hope to the poor, announcing life and its fullness and denouncing the poverty and repression that brought death to so many of his beloved people. Romero called on all the people of El Salvador to participate in bringing to fullness the peace and justice that are signs of God's reign. And he did so with such a coherence and credibility that in the end he became the good news that he proclaimed. In the words of another Salvadoran martyr, Ignacio Ellacuría, "With Archbishop Romero, God has visited El Salvador."[35]

The first three months that Romero served as archbishop of San Salvador laid the foundation for the remaining three years, until his martyrdom on March 24, 1980. The death of Rutilio Grande, instead of being the reason to draw back and reconsider options that placed the church — and indeed his own life — in danger, occasioned instead the defining first step in a journey that would lead finally to Romero's martyrdom.

Strengthened by his relationship to the people, Romero began to define the mission of the church in the midst of a conflictive social reality in the weeks that followed. On Holy Thursday, within a few weeks of Grande's death, he told the people:

> *You are prophets in the world.... You have to announce like the prophets — like a prophetic people anointed by the Spirit that anointed Christ — the wonders of God in the world, to encourage the good that is done in the world and also to energetically denounce evil.*[36]

He called on the people, not to be spectators, but to allow their hearts to enter deeply into the tradition of the church and to find their home there, a sentiment that would one day be etched on his tomb in San Salvador: *"Sentir con la Iglesia."*

> *The Word of God has a religious mission...and a human mission: to love our neighbor means to be concerned about their needs, their concrete situation, and, like the Good Samaritan, to help the poor fallen by the roadside.*[37]

Romero was more and more clearly defining one of the signs that would characterize his spirituality: to love one's neighbor means concretely to come to the aid of the poor who have been beaten, robbed, and left by the roadside, and to denounce the cause of their violation.

Romero's spirituality was also deeply rooted in the paschal mystery, uniting the mystery of the dying and rising of Christ with the death and resurrection of the Salvadoran people. On Good Friday the same year he said:

> *Now that we are together at the tomb of Christ, awaiting his resurrection, we are examining our life, our commitments to him. We do not want to be Judases. We do not want to be cowardly apostles. We want to be faithful from now on. The hour demands it.*[38]

In the weeks that followed Rutilio Grande's death, Romero began to define the characteristics of a church that accompanies the passion of Christ in the passion of its people:

> *The church is concerned about the rights of people...and about life that is at risk.... The church is concerned about those who cannot speak, those who suffer, those who are tortured, those who are silenced. This is not getting involved in politics. But when politics begins to "touch the altar," the church has the right to speak.*
>
> *Let this be clear: when the church preaches social justice, equality, and the dignity of people, defending those who suffer and those who are assaulted, this is not subversion; this is not Marxism. This is the authentic teaching of the church.*[39]

And, Romero added, *"The church cannot remain silent. It has to speak out."*

Just two months after Rutilio Grande's death, Father Alfonso Navarro was assassinated by gunmen in his parish in San Salvador. Once again, Romero would make of his funeral Mass an occasion to encourage the people of El Salvador to continue their pilgrimage with faith. In a phrase that equally describes Romero's journey until his martyrdom, Romero told the people:

> They say that a desert caravan, led by a Bedouin, was desperate with thirst and looked for water in the mirages of the desert. The Bedouin guided them, "Not there, but here." This happened several times. Finally, somebody got annoyed, took out a pistol, and shot the Bedouin. In his agony, the Bedouin stretched out his hand and said, "Not there, but here." And so he died, pointing the way.[40]

According to an eyewitness, Navarro died forgiving his assassins. Romero encouraged the people to find in Navarro's death *"a new impulse of hope, of joy . . . for those of us who continue this pilgrimage."* Instead of an incitation to further violence, he encouraged them to see an invitation to *"a new force of love in the church."*

However, the violence escalated. In May, the army occupied Rutilio Grande's parish in Aguilares, killing the sacristan, expelling a foreign priest, and turning the church into a military barracks. In June, Romero returned to Aguilares to reclaim the parish. There he told the nervous crowd that had gathered in the church:

> Today it is my responsibility to assemble this church. This sanctuary has been profaned, the tabernacle for the Blessed Sacrament has been destroyed, and the people have been humiliated and sacrificed in such an undignified manner. . . .
> I bring you the Word Christ sends you: a word of solidarity, a word of encouragement and orientation, and, finally, a word of conversion.[41]

Once again Romero reaffirmed the commitment he had made to the poor of El Salvador at the Mass in the cathedral three months before. In a phrase that would characterize the paschal character of his spirituality, he referred to the poor who had gathered in the parish of Aguilares as a crucified people:

You are the image...of Christ, nailed to the cross and lanced by the spear. You are a symbol of every town, like Aguilares, that will be struck down and trampled upon; but if you suffer with faith and give your suffering a redemptive meaning, Aguilares will be singing the precious song of liberation.[42]

Romero pointed to the redemptive significance of the suffering of his people, not in a passive way — as victims — but rather as inspired Christians participating with the Spirit of the Gospel in the liberation of their people:

Let us be firm in defending our rights, but with great love in our hearts, because to defend our rights in this way we are also seeking the conversion of sinners. This is the vengeance of the Christian.[43]

The depth of Romero's spiritual life could be glimpsed whenever he spoke about the price of conformity and the price of conversion. Speaking of conformity he said,

It is forgotten that mediocrity will always be majority and the courage of authenticity minority. Recall "the wide way" and "the narrow way" of the Gospel. How necessary in this difficult hour is a conscience docile to the Lord's truth. In this difficult hour more than ever is there need for prayer united with a genuine will to be converted, prayer that out of intimacy with God cuts one off from the confused clamor of life's shallow experiences, a will to be converted that is not afraid to lose prestige or privilege, or to change a way of thinking when it is seen that Christ insists on a new way of thinking that is more in keeping with his Gospel.[44]

Conversion from social conformity to the authenticity of truth is costly. Cautioned to be more diplomatic, more accommodating, less upsetting, Romero said:

Some want to keep a Gospel so disembodied that it doesn't get involved at all in the world it must save. Christ is now in history. Christ is in the womb of the people. Christ is now bringing about a new heaven and a new earth.[45]

Oscar Romero lived and died an authentic Christian who laid down his life out of love for the poor.

2

The Historical Demands
of the Gospel

Our world in El Salvador is not an abstraction.... It is a world which, in its vast majority, is composed of poor and oppressed men and women. And it is the same world of the poor that provides us the key to understand our Christian faith.... The poor tell us what our world is really like, and what the mission of the church should be.[1]

Seven weeks before his death, Archbishop Romero was invited to give an address, which he titled "The Political Dimension of Faith," at the University of Louvain in Belgium. It was a manifesto of his faith. He did not confuse politics with spirituality or theology. Rather he insisted that there is a political dimension to spirituality, just as there is a political dimension to the Gospel.

Romero began his address at Louvain by differentiating between the world of people living in developed countries like Belgium and the United States and those of "the world of the poor" living in Third World countries like El Salvador or in pockets of misery in the First World. Romero found in the poor "the key" to understanding what the world is really like and what the mission of the church should be:

Experiencing these realities, and letting ourselves be affected by them, far from separating us from our faith, has sent us back to the world of the poor as to our true home. It has moved us, as a first, basic step, to take the world of the poor upon ourselves. It is there that we have found the real faces of the poor.... There we have met farmworkers without land and without steady employment, without running water or electricity in their homes, without medical assistance when mothers give birth, and without schools for their children. There we met factory workers who have no labor rights and who get fired from their jobs if they demand such rights, human beings who are at the mercy of cold economic calculations. There we have met the mothers and wives of those who have disappeared or who are political prisoners. There we met the shantytown dwellers whose wretchedness defies imagination, suffering the permanent mockery of the mansions nearby.[2]

What did Romero mean by "the face of the poor"? Precisely he meant the face of those who suffer, endure, and resist. That is, the face of those involved in land takeovers and labor disputes, of those captured, disappeared, and assassinated by the death squads and security forces. In the context of this world Romero tried to discern "the signs of the time" and, like the Bedouin in the desert, point out to the people the way to go: "Not there, but here."

This is the world in which Romero lived and toward which he turned his attention as archbishop. This is the world into which the church of El Salvador moved, making the poor the heart of its pastoral ministry and ultimately sharing the fate of the poor. *"Anyone committed to the poor must suffer the same fate as the poor. And in El Salvador we know the fate of the poor: to be taken away, to be tortured, to be jailed, to be found dead."*[3]

It is important to emphasize the active dimension of Oscar Romero's spirituality. Certainly the church has lived among the poor for centuries, and the poor have been both the majority of its faithful and the primary object of its charity. What is unique in Romero's case is that he invited the poor themselves to expose the truth about the historical reality in which they lived, revealing both the structural dimension of oppression and its tragic consequences. Romero refused to ameliorate the desperation of the poor with charity. Rather he believed in their liberation and deliverance to freedom. *"The church invokes the freedom of people...as the architect of their own destiny to choose their own way to achieve the destiny that God points out to them."*[4]

Romero also encouraged the poor to reveal the Gospel dimension of their historical reality. The poor are the geography of God's incarnation in history, the sacrament of Christ suffering today.

> *It is within this world devoid of a human face, this contemporary sacrament of the suffering servant of Yahweh, that the church of my archdiocese has undertaken to incarnate itself....I am well aware how much in this regard is left to be done. But I say it with immense joy, for we have made the effort not to pass by...not to circle round the one lying wounded in the roadway, but to approach him or her as did the Good Samaritan.*[5]

Day after day, poor farmers and workers were assaulted, tortured, disappeared, or assassinated when they protested their conditions of poverty; and those who came to their defense, as Rutilio Grande had done, shared the same fate as those they defended. To be a Good Samaritan in El Salvador ultimately meant to risk being counted among the tortured and disfigured persons abandoned by the roadside.

In his address at the University of Louvain, Oscar Romero said, *"Our encounter with the poor has regained for us the central truth of the Gospel, through which the Word of God urges us to conversion,"* conversion to the poor. The poor are the key to *"what the world is really like,"* and to *"what the mission of the church should be."*[6]

> *This is my greatest concern: to try to build with Christ a church according to his heart....For that reason I ask you to focus not only on the weekly events that the prophetic mission of the church obliges me to illuminate, but on the light that illuminates, on the attempt of this poor pastor to build a church according to the heart of God.*[7]

For Romero, building a church according to the heart of God meant building a church which beat with the heart of the poor. This was the good news that he preached — the church sought to make its heart one with the people. He proclaimed the Gospel as one who knew the world of the poor, saw the world from their eyes, and shared their sufferings and hopes, and as one who knew the heart of God and God's compassion for the poor.

Not only was Romero a prophet of God's Word; such was his relation to the people that he could say: *"The people are my prophet."*[8] He not only preached the Word of God to the people; he listened to the Word with the heart of the poor, with their hopes and joys, their sorrow and anguish, and walked with them as he helped them discern the way ahead:

> *The people of God, illuminated by their faith, look at their own aspirations, demands, and ideals. And with this faith they know how to discern what God wants according to the signs of the time. Clearly not everything that people demand is the Word of God, but in the heart of the demands of our moment there is much of God to be found, and here we have to discern.*[9]

Romero believed that the poor unmasked the powerful and showed the church what it should become. He understood that the church became holy inside the gritty contest between good and evil. The gift of Oscar Romero to the church, and to the world, is that he transformed — by his spirituality and his ministry — the very meaning of the true marks of the church. The church, he insisted, is one, holy, catholic, and apostolic by union with Christ and its accompaniment of the poor, by its fidelity to the Gospel proclaimed as good news to the poor, by its mission of evangelization to defend the life of the poor and to promote justice, and by the testimony of its martyrs to bear witness to God's love. Romero spoke of the incompleteness of the church's incarnation of these true marks and asked pardon of the people for the church's failure to fully make these signs take flesh.

He knew that the church too sins and challenged us to accept a church slow to be purified. The church of El Salvador was not "one," but deeply divided like the society it reflected. Even within the popular organizations and base Christian communities there were serious theological and political disagreements. If the church is "apostolic" in its mission, to whom is it sent? The "catholicity" of the church was often insular, parochial, and defensive. Definitions of "holiness" were too often an expression of ideological preferences. The church is holy and unholy, a grace and an obstacle to grace, a sacrament and a scandal. The church is flawed and sacred like the humanity for which it exists. The church is, like us, both a vessel of redemption and in need of redemption. For this reason Romero called the church to a deeper conversion to the poor where false gods are unmasked and where the good news is received and enfleshed.

On the tomb of martyred Father Octavio Ortiz are engraved two questions, taken from Jesus' inaugural proclamation in the synagogue in Nazareth: "What does it mean to preach liberty to the oppressed?" "What does it mean to give sight to the blind?" These questions were the basis of the retreat that Octavio Ortiz directed with a group of young people the morning he and four others were so brutally killed by the National Guard. As if they could not kill him enough, the soldiers rolled a tank over Octavio's body, disfiguring his face. His assassination was an indication of just how subversive the Word of God had become in El Salvador.

> *A very tragic day. It dawned with the news that there had been a military operation in El Despertar in the parish of San Antonio Abad. It was at a house frequently used for retreats designed to deepen the participants' Christian faith. Father Octavio Ortiz, along with Sister Chepita, as they call the Belgian sister who works there, was leading a program of introduction to the Christian life for some forty young men. But at dawn today, the National Guard, with a riot squad, set off a bomb to break down the door and then entered violently with armored cars and shooting. Father Octavio, when he realized what was happening, got up just to meet his death, as did four other young men. The rest*

*of the group, including two women religious, were taken to
the headquarters of the National Guard. We did not learn
about the murders of Father Octavio and the other four
young men until the afternoon, when their bodies already
had been taken to the morgue at the cemetery. Father Octavio's face was very disfigured; it looked like it had been
run over and flattened by something very heavy.... In my
homily [at the funeral Mass].... I analyzed the crime perpe-
trated against Father Octavio and the four who had been
sacrificed with him. I called for a rational response rather
than resorting to violence and force. I protested this attack
on the dignity of our church.*[10]

The challenge that Octavio Ortiz faced was the same challenge that Romero faced, a challenge that Gustavo Gutiérrez
describes as follows: "How do we tell the poor that God really
loves them?"[11] In other words, "Is the Gospel really good news?"
The remarkable thing about Romero's proclamation of the Gospel each week was that — judged by the frequent applause of the
poor who listened — he really did proclaim good news to the
poor. Why was this so? The simple answer is that the poor really
felt the Gospel was addressed to them in the context of their
lives and struggle. They really heard in Romero's proclamation
a message of hope that spoke to their hearts:

*It is something new among our people that today the poor
see in the church a source of hope and a support for their
noble struggle for liberation. The hope that our church en-
courages is neither naïve nor passive. It is rather a summons
from the word of God for the great majority of the people,
the poor, that they assume their proper responsibility, that
they understand their own conscientization, that in a country where it is legally or practically prohibited ... they set
about organizing themselves. And it is support, sometimes
critical support, for their just causes and demands. The
hope that we preach to the poor is intended to give them
back their dignity, to encourage them to take charge of their
own future.*[12]

Of course the preaching of a Gospel that endorsed the cause of those who are persecuted would be understood as a "political" reading by the persecutors themselves and by those who sought neutrality in the face of such injustice. Such a Gospel would be good news, however, to those who suffered. Romero insisted that the Gospel be read from the perspective of the downtrodden, who were the anchor of God's Word. Without them the Gospel was a pacification, an amelioration, a lie. More than that, he said the Gospel lived only if and when people of faith incarnated it — that God needed human beings to enflesh hope even in the midst of an agony imposed on them by those who "killed" the spirit of the Gospel and used it to endorse injustice:

> *We not only read the Bible, we analyze it, we celebrate it, we incarnate it in our reality, we want to make it our life. This is the meaning of the homily: to incarnate the Word of God in our people. This is not politics. When we point out the political, social, and economic sins in the homily, this is the Word of God incarnate in our reality, a reality that often does not reflect the reign of God but rather sin. We proclaim the Gospel to point out to people the paths of redemption.*[13]

This word was both Word of God and word of the people. Romero could say with credibility:

> *My word is not mine but the Word of God. And if it reaches the hearts of many who need light, consolation, joy, hope, this is no virtue of mine. It is God who by means of my homily is communicating the grace of our Lord Jesus Christ.*[14]

With equal credibility he could also say:

> *We want to be the voice of those who have no voice, in order to cry out against every assault of our human rights so that justice is done.*[15]

Recalling Jesus' inaugural proclamation in the synagogue at Nazareth, "The Spirit of the Lord has anointed me to preach good news to the poor" (Luke 4:16ff.), Romero said:

In the most sublime homily ever proclaimed, Christ closes the book and says: "Today these things have been fulfilled." This is the homily: the Word of God is not a reading of the past but a living Word, a Spirit that is being accomplished here and now.[16]

Romero had become like his people — radically, imaginatively alive in the midst of a holocaust, trusting the Word to transform a situation that grew grimmer each day. Whatever overwhelming pressures mounted at his archdiocesan doors, he held to the anchor of a Gospel that promised to be good news to those who suffered. His mission was simple: to preach that good news to the poor until his voice fell. Romero was the mediator between the Word of God and the word of his people, between the call of God and the cry of the poor. In this role he grounded his spirituality, and in this way he fulfilled his mission as both pastor and prophet:

This is the mission of Christ, to bring the good news to the poor, to those who receive only bad news, to those who feel only the assault of the powerful, to those who see the riches that make others happy pass them by; to these the Lord has come.[17]

The church has not only incarnated itself in the world of the poor, giving them hope; it has also firmly committed itself to their defense. The majority of the poor in our country are oppressed and repressed daily by economic and political structures. The terrible words spoken by the prophets of Israel continue to be verified among us. Among us there are those who sell others for money, who sell a poor person for a pair of sandals.[18]

Just as Romero's spirituality cannot be understood apart from the historical context in which he lived — a history characterized by conflict and violence, by structures of oppression and movements of liberation — so, too, his spirituality cannot be understood apart from a preferential option for the poor, what he calls *"the most fundamental characteristic of our faith."* It cannot be emphasized enough that such an option is not merely a socio-political option, one among many that might be chosen; it is, at its root, a theological option essential to faith:

> *Where the poor begin to really live, where the poor begin to free themselves, where persons are able to sit around a common table to share with one another — the God of life is there. When the church inserts itself into the socio-political world, it does so in order to work with it so that by such cooperation life may be given to the poor. In doing so, therefore, it is not distancing itself from its mission, nor is it doing something of secondary importance or something incidental to its mission. It is giving testimony to its faith in God; it is being the instrument of the Spirit, the Lord and Giver of Life.*[19]

The poor are not only central to the spirituality of Romero; they are the key to what the world is really like and what the mission of the church should be:

> *The world of the poor teaches us what the nature of Christian love is, a love that certainly seeks peace, but also unmasks false pacifism — the pacifism of resignation and inactivity. It is a love that should certainly be freely offered, but that seeks to be effective in history. The world of the poor teaches us that the sublimity of Christian love ought to be mediated through the overriding necessity of justice for the majority. It ought not to turn away from honorable conflict. The world of the poor teaches us that liberation will arrive only when the poor are not simply on the receiving end of handouts from governments or from the churches, but when they themselves are the masters and protagonists of their own struggle and liberation.*[20]

Romero spoke of defending the poor as a necessary conse-quence of incarnating the church in the world of the poor. This choice, which came to be characterized as the church's "preferential option for the poor," is at the heart of the church's mission and comprises the political dimension of faith:

> *Incarnation in the sociopolitical world of the poor is the locus for deepening faith in God and in his Christ. We believe in Jesus, who came to bring the fullness of life, and we believe in a living God, who gives life to men and women and wants them truly to live. These radical truths of the faith become really true and truly radical when the church enters into the heart of the life and death of its people. Then there is put before the faith of the church, as it is put before the faith of every individual, the most fundamental choice: to be in favor of life or to be in favor of death.*[21]

The Gospel that Romero proclaimed was never *"an opiate of the people,"* but *"the very heart of God in a heartless world."* His heart, in turn, was profoundly moved by the sufferings of the poor:

> *As a pastor and as a Salvadoran citizen, I am profoundly ashamed that the organized sector of our people continue to be massacred, simply because they are protesting in the streets for justice and freedom. I am sure that so much blood shed and so much pain caused to the families of so many victims will not be in vain.*[22]

Romero had a keen sense of the demonic power of sin that permeated the dominant economic and political structures of Salvadoran society. These structures, like the "principalities and powers" cited by St. Paul in his epistles, demanded absolute obedience. The unleashed violence which targeted the organized poor was a direct result of the need to protect the structures of privilege that favored the wealthy landowners. Romero could have denounced the physical violence while accepting the inevitability of such structural inequality as if the two forms of violence were not linked. But authenticity demanded that he denounce the structural roots of the violence as well. He could not be obedient to God and obedient to the status quo. He held only God as an absolute, and he demanded disobedience to any law, government, or army that violated the people. Romero was "sacrilegious" because he didn't offer allegiance to the "Fatherland," as the right referred to the state. Few bishops have been as clear and unequivocal in standing before the power of government and the armed forces:

> *We see with great clarity that here neutrality is impossible.*
> *...And here what is most fundamental about the faith is*
> *given expression in history: either we believe in a God of*
> *life, or we serve the idols of death.*[23]

Perhaps from the point of view of the powerful his more egregious "sin" was to have believed that the poor had a right to organize and defend themselves.

> *Nobody can violate the right to organize....it is a human*
> *right. The demands that these organizations make are just,*
> *and they must be heard. The point is not to repress a*
> *demonstration that is asking for justice but to listen to what*
> *is being said in order to attend to the cry of this large sector*
> *of our people for the sake of the common good. For that*
> *reason Christ also supports what is just, and defends it....*
> *It is not a sin to organize....For a Christian the sin is to*
> *lose the perspective of God.*[24]

Evangelization had to include both pastoral response and prophetic proclamation, personal compassion and structural transformation. Romero's definition of sin cuts like a sword through ambiguity, rationalization, the reasonableness of business as usual, the need for order, the need to protect national security or maximize profits. Sin, personal or structural, is that which sucks the life out of the defenseless whether the oppression is indirect or immediate.

> *It is not a matter of sheer routine that I insist once again*
> *on the existence in our country of structures of sin. They*
> *are sinful because they produce the fruits of sin: the deaths*

*of Salvadorans — the swift death brought by repression or
the long, drawn out, but no less real, death from structural
oppression. That is why we have denounced what in our
country has become the idolatry of wealth, of the absolute
right, within the capitalist system, of private property, of
political power in national security regimes, in the name of
which personal security is itself institutionalized.*[25]

One of the legacies of Archbishop Romero's prophetic presence among the poor was the discovery that the poor, in fact,
evangelize us. Eva, a woman religious who worked directly with
the refugees, offered an insight to the values of the poor that
shaped the spirituality of Romero as well as her own, a spirituality that responded to the historical demands of the Gospel: "I
am impressed above all by their forgiveness," she said, speaking
of the refugees. "They have a great capacity to forgive, something that is difficult for us. A mother might say that her third
son was killed yesterday, and in the celebration of the Word she
prays from her heart for her enemies, asking God to change their
hearts and to take away what blinds them."

The refugees had a great capacity to suffer. They did not let
themselves become discouraged, but were convinced that the pe-
riod of trial was only one step on the journey. Eva told this story
of forgiveness and hope: "A woman I know fled to another town
with her six children when her husband was killed by a paramilitary group. When she came to the refugee camp she met another
woman, also a widow, with seven children, whose husband had
been a member of the same paramilitary group that killed the first
woman's husband. To my amazement, the first woman gave what
food she had to the second woman and her family."

For Eva, the poor are a profound source of renewal for her religious vocation: "I believe this experience with the refugees has
been a great opportunity to rediscover my vocation, to find meaning in community life, to live more poorly, to follow Jesus, and to
live a more intense life of prayer."[26] Archbishop Romero was another source of renewal for Eva's religious vocation — a vocation
tested by the divisions within the church.

When the war was beginning, Eva had been a Carmelite sister for twenty-five years. As the persecution mounted, she chose to accompany a base Christian community of peasants and workers. When she and the four other sisters involved in this parish pastoral work were told by their superior to cease such work because it could mean military retaliations against the religious order, Eva and her sisters went to Archbishop Romero to ask him what to do. They explained to him that they had reached a point where they would have to choose the Carmelites or the poor. Romero listened carefully. "He said we needed to be light and salt within the congregation. He said that only we could decide what we must do. However, he said the poor must be evangelized."[27]

After that, Romero offered them the silence of the chapel in which to discern God's will and suggested they read a Scripture passage he thought might assist them. When Eva, who is a very soft-spoken woman, tells the next part of the story, she still laughs. The passage he gave us was from Luke 4:16ff.:

> The Spirit of the Lord is upon me, because he has anointed me to preach good news to the poor. He has sent me to proclaim release of the captives and recovery of sight to the blind, to set at liberty those who are oppressed, to announce the acceptable year of the Lord.

And so the sisters decided to leave their religious order and form a new community of sisters who were not canonically vowed. The sisters, however, chose to take their vows before their base Christian community. Eva remembers the woman who made her a red dress, the dress of the people, that would replace her Carmelite habit. "That woman, Cecelia, was a young catechist. She was later murdered by the army — they cut out her tongue and her eyes."[28]

When the sisters took their vows — of obedience (to be faithful to the poor in their midst), chastity (to remain available to the community as their family), and poverty (to live as the people lived) — the bishop who witnessed their vows was Oscar Romero. "What a day it was," says Eva, "a day of joy and dancing, and there in our midst was Monseñor Romero." Romero had only one concern that day. It was not that religious sisters were leaving their order or that he would receive further criticism from the nuncio for presiding at the founding of noncanonical orders. His only question, Eva said, was addressed to the many peasants of Guazapa that had gathered to "receive" the sisters' vows. "He asked everyone gathered there if we women had been a witness to them."[29]

Romero's spirituality included but went beyond the church as institution and embraced the Spirit present in the people. He was humbled by his blindness to his people's needs before he was thrust into the inferno of the war as their spiritual leader. He struggled to understand the concrete unfolding of the people's journey during the war, especially as the violence intensified and popular organizations and Christian base community groups groped for ways to resist the brutality of the security forces.

Romero was not always certain about what strategy of the church would be most effective. Already by 1978, with the publication of his third pastoral letter, *The Church and Popular Political Organizations,* Romero had formulated a defense of his people's right and obligation to organize and plead their own cause for justice. In the letter, which was also signed by Bishop Arturo Rivera y Damas, his successor and the only bishop who supported him, Romero wrote:

> The church has a mission to serve the people.... The church's role is to defend the cause of the poor and all that is human in the people's struggle. The church identifies with the poor when they demand their legitimate rights. In our country the right they are demanding is hardly more than the right to survive, to escape from misery.[30]

Romero's defense of popular organizations was not only, or even primarily, a political option, but was also an essential part of evangelization. He quotes Paul VI's apostolic exhortation *Evangelii Nuntiandi* to make this point:

> The church has the duty to proclaim the liberation of millions of human beings, many of whom are its own children,

the duty of assisting the birth of this liberation, of giving witness to it, of ensuring that it is complete. This is not foreign to evangelization.[31]

This defense of popular organizations in El Salvador meant that *"faith and politics ought to be united in a Christian who has a political vocation, but they are not to be identified.... Faith ought to inspire political action, but not be mistaken for it."*[32]

Romero's concern, however, was not limited to the church. He found the Spirit also active beyond the visible structures and witness of the church:

There is a more fundamental connection, based on faith, between the church and popular organizations, even if they do not profess to be Christian. The church believes that the action of the Spirit who brings Christ to life in human beings is greater than itself. Far beyond the confines of the church, Christ's redemption is powerfully at work.... The church tries to see the popular organizations in this way in order to purify them, encourage them, and incorporate them, together with the efforts of Christians, into the overall plan of Christ's redemption.[33]

He was clear about his allies: the poor and those who un-equivocally took the side of the poor, whether Christian or not. Romero, in fact, encouraged the founding of two popular organizations: one was the Mothers of the Disappeared; the other, the Non-Governmental Human Rights Commission of El Salvador, founded in 1978 to document the escalating violence against civilians.

This organization, composed of Salvadoran citizens, initially used archdiocesan office space, where its team gathered documentation listing the human rights abuses, which they then relayed to the United Nations Commission on Human Rights in Geneva.

Imagine the task of those who daily had to hear heart-rending testimonies or take detailed photographs of bodies that had been horribly mutilated. Their work was a chamber of horrors, and it had consequences. Those who publicly spoke the truth or documented it, like Oscar Romero, became targets of the same repression. One by one seven members of the Non-Governmental Human Rights Commission were assassinated. Marianella García Villas, the first president of the commission, was tortured and killed as she accompanied refugees in Guazapa. Five other members of the commission, Joaquín Cáceres, Miguel Angel Montenegro, Rafael Terezón, Reynaldo Blanco, and Herbert Anaya, were captured, tortured, and then sent to prison. Rev. Bill Hutchinson, who worked with the Commission during the war, described their ordeal:

> They were choked to the point of asphyxiation and beaten on the face and body with clenched fists. They were hit on the testicles and about the ears. They were thrown to the floor with their hands cuffed behind their backs, then lifted by their arms until they felt their shoulders were being pulled from their sockets. They were kept standing for days on end and deprived of sleep as threats were hurled against their families.[34]

Torture isn't only physical; its deeper aim is to break the spirit. Whose bravery could endure isolation, threats to their families, the constant insinuation of the hollowness of one's cause? Commission member Miguel Angel Montenegro described the dynamic:

> As for me, I was brutally tortured — physically and psychologically — to break me. The physical is less harmful than the psychological. You are in a dark place. You are isolated.... My mom came to visit me at the Treasury Police, and I told her that I had resigned myself to die.[35]

Herbert Anaya, who was the second president of the commission, explained to his torturers what *their* options were. The discourse on death was vintage Anaya.

> I told them...that I was well aware...that the worst they could do to me was kill me, and that this was not a problem

because, if they killed me, it would be my body, and my soul would continue to work for justice.[36]

For Herbert Anaya, the decision to stay in El Salvador after his release from prison was an ultimate act of accompaniment. Anaya faced the executioners with an audacity that took even Salvadorans, literate in the grammar of terror, by surprise. In a television debate, Herbert Anaya openly accused the head of the National Police, Reynaldo López Nuila, of lies and brutal repression. Nobody, nobody made such accusations in public without paying a price. Herbert Anaya's understanding of accompaniment was not spiritualized, but profoundly empathetic and backed by action. Within months, on October 26, 1987, the death squads came for him. He was shot outside his house as his children prepared to go to school.

Weeks before he was killed Anaya had said publicly, "The agony of not working for justice is stronger than the certain possibility of my death. This latter is but one instant; the other is one's whole life."[37] Like Marianella García, Herbert Anaya was not part of the church that carried forward the work of Archbishop Romero. He was not a "religious" person, nor was he simply a documenter of atrocities. He stood up to the army in defense of the people. Like Romero, Marianella and Herbert were holy people. Romero never saw the reign of God as limited to Catholicism or Christianity. He had seen the church's failure and the courage of those outside it:

> *Everyone who struggles for justice, everyone who makes just claims in unjust surroundings is working for God's reign even though not a Christian. The church does not comprise all of God's reign; God's reign goes beyond church boundaries.*[38]

Herbert Anaya's spirituality was marked by the same fire that consumed Romero: love of the people and a love for justice. That love drove them both. They carried the people's suffering in their hearts. Both were imbued with the *mística* of the liberation process. Romero, in fact, often found *more* holiness outside

Catholicism. This insight from so orthodox a priest must have been discovered in the depths of a heart intrinsically linked to the people's spirit, the Spirit of life, that embraced them all in the heart of darkness.

> *Outside the limits of Catholicism perhaps there is more faith, more holiness. So we must not extinguish the Spirit. The Spirit is not the monopoly of a movement, even a Christian movement, of a hierarchy or priesthood or religious congregation. The Spirit is free.*[39]

The passionate spirit of love for his people that drove Anaya left him utterly vulnerable like the people he defended. To not act for justice was worse than death. Anaya and Romero were two very different people: one an extrovert, humorous, charming, with an intense nature; the other circumspect, reserved, a pastor who could not abandon the poor. Both men faced what the rest of us block from consciousness: death itself. Anaya was clear: the death of his soul was too high a price to pay for a life of silence.

The irrepressible spirit of Herbert Anaya touched people deeply. In a very real sense, he resurrected their spirit. After Romero's funeral, the streets of El Salvador were cleared of protests, marches, and gatherings that expressed the people's voice — any voice except that of the army or the president. No organization, except the courageous Mothers of the Disappeared, dared take to the streets for fear of capture or death. But Anaya's death in 1987 occasioned a reclaiming of the streets by the popular organizations, opening space for a genuine democratic voice. His assassination had angered people to a risky defiance. To openly come to the cathedral for Anaya's funeral Mass and to accompany the body to the cemetery was to invite jeopardy. Anaya's wife, Mirna, describes the popular sentiment at that time:

> It was pretty strange in those days. There was an effervescence in the popular movement, a strange strength, full of a lot of anger, but with decisiveness not to allow the murder

of my husband to go unprotested. I never thought so many people would come to the cathedral.... Very poor people came ... donating all the money they had.[40]

Despite the presence of soldiers armed with M-16s, hundreds of people processed openly through the streets behind Anaya's coffin. The sheer numbers intimidated the army. In death as in life, Herbert Anaya had created an opening. The people were resurrected in the streets of San Salvador. Never again would the popular organizations allow the space of popular protest to be closed.

Herbert Anaya left five children. Should he have been less vigorous in his denunciations? Should he have remained alive for his children? His young son Neto seems to understand that death doesn't kill, fear does. For Neto and his brother and sisters, who still cry for their funny and tender father, the fact, not the metaphor, is that Herbert Anaya lives. Neto's poem for his father says simply:

> His blood was spilled,
> but he is alive,
> alive where they can't hurt him
> alive in the hearts of my people.[41]

Herbert Anaya's life and death point to love and justice as the task that makes us human.

In his fourth and final pastoral letter, *The Church's Mission amid the National Crisis,* written in 1979, Romero reminds us that the mission of the church is:

to be the voice of the voiceless, a defender of the rights of the poor, a promoter of every just aspiration for liberation, a guide, an empowerer, a humanizer of every legitimate struggle to achieve a more just society, a society that prepares the way for the true kingdom of God in history.

This demands of the church a greater presence among the poor. It ought to be in solidarity with them, running the risks they run, enduring the persecution that is their

*fate, ready to give the greatest possible testimony to its love
by defending and promoting those who were first in Jesus'
love.*[42]

Romero's role as archbishop cast him, at a critical historical
moment, as the church's public voice in the midst of a fratricidal
war. But it is not simply history that explains Romero's canonization by the people or that explains why the people claim
him as one who speaks for them as their beloved Monseñor.
It is a spirituality that embodied the witness of Jesus of Nazareth, who proclaimed love, especially of the dispossessed, as the
sign of God's sojourn among us. This "good news" is not a new
proclamation. Living it and dying it, however, is good news that
undermines the tragic cynicism of our age. Romero did not simply proclaim good news to the poor; he proclaimed that the poor
themselves, not poverty, are God's good news.

*We do not praise poverty for itself. We praise the poor as
the sign, the sacrament of God in the world.*[43]

The more Romero discovered the deep spiritual life of the
poor, the more he discovered the God of life. Defense of the poor
made bold a shy man whose courage to confront the idols of
wealth and power became the gift of the Salvadoran church to
the world. Romero's courage was the people's gift to him, and he
did not hesitate to say it:

*God knows how hard it was for me to come here to the
capital. How timid I have felt before you, except for the
support that you as church, have given me. You have made
your archbishop a sign of Christianity.*[44]

The essence of Romero's spirituality was that he clung to
the God of love and refused to bow before the idols of death.
Whether the false gods were the state, ideology, power, or wealth,
he did not waver in his fidelity to a God of the world's castoffs.
Romero took on the merchants of death in El Salvador, as well
as a global system that condemned the poor:

I denounce especially the absolutizing of wealth. This is the great evil in El Salvador: wealth, private property, as an untouchable absolute. Woe to the one who touches that high tension wire. It burns.[45]

The God of the prophets is uncompromising. And so was Romero.

3

The Heart of the Poor

Is there no balm in Gilead, is there no physician there? Why then has the health of my poor people not been restored? Oh, that my head were a spring of water, and my eyes a fountain of tears so that I might weep day and night for the slain of my poor people. (Jer. 8:22; 9:1)

When efforts to protect the people had failed, when the hideous became commonplace, when children and the elderly were targets of grotesque counterinsurgency violations, Oscar Romero reclaimed an ancient spiritual practice: accompaniment. Imagine the dark night of the soul a pastor experiences watching his people dragged off, raped, tortured, strangled, and beaten to death daily. One thousand a month were killed in 1980. None of Romero's efforts could stop the flow of blood. The temptation to despair was real. Grappling with his own impotence and the apparent triumph of evil, Romero called upon the Salvadoran church to offer the only gift it could — itself. Powerless, disgraced, ignored, persecuted, this church, nevertheless, could walk with people and be present as they walked the *via dolorosa*. Such faithfulness could not prevent suffering but could, in its act of solidarity, bear witness, the essence of accompaniment. This was the church's gift to the people, just as this crucified people's faithfulness to God was its gift to the church.

What then is a spirituality of accompaniment? In a word, it is a spirituality imbued with the spirit of the poor.

Since the 1960s, liberation theology had challenged the church and transformed history. It taught not a new Gospel but an incarnated Gospel — one people lived. The Gospel, long the province of professional clerics, was for the first time read and interpreted by the poor. In Romero's words:

The poor have shown the church the true way to go. A church that does not join the poor, in order to speak out from the side of the poor against the injustices committed against them, is not the true church of Jesus Christ.[1]

Archbishop Romero was not alone in experiencing a deeper conversion to the poor of his tortured country. During the war years, many missionaries, clerics, Salvadoran professionals, and foreign nationals experienced a rekindling of their flagging faith in their encounter with the church of the poor. In this encounter, many discovered not only a hunger for justice but a hunger for God. Such a spiritual awakening occurred not in a monastery, convent, or church but in a countryside under bombardment, among people running for their lives through ravines and tall canefields, hiding under the ceiba trees from the gun-sights of bombers or machine gunners. It was the peasant and worker church that revealed a spirituality that no longer fit the classic models of spirituality. It burst the wineskins of individual holiness and revealed the spiritual path of a people.

Unfortunately, brothers and sisters, we are the product of a spiritualized, individualistic education. We are taught: try to save your soul and don't worry about the rest. We told those who suffered: be patient, heaven will follow, hang on. No, that's not right, that's not salvation![2]

Salvation was for those who dared enter history, who dared accompany those without protection. Accompaniment is a post-modern spirituality and a very ancient one. In the deserts, wastelands, and killing fields of this world, adrift with refugees and exiles, accompaniment is an act of faith in both the destiny of the poor and the Spirit of God who journeys with the castoffs. During the war years in El Salvador, the God of life accompanied those who fled death, seeking freedom from tyranny.

The following two stories are taken from *Letter to the Churches*, a biweekly publication of the Jesuit University in San Salvador, which began to publish its newsletter one year after Romero's martyrdom. In no small measure, these letters have helped to keep alive Romero's spirituality, which mirrors so faithfully the spirituality of the poor. As the poor responded from the depths of their souls to the historical demands of the Gospel, so did Romero.

Teresa's story exemplifies the spirit of the Salvadoran poor. She is a young nurse. Years ago, during the war, when Teresa still lived in San Salvador, she was assaulted by two security agents in civilian dress. They took her to a vacant lot and savagely raped her until she lost consciousness. When she woke up the next morning she had only fifteen cents in her pocket. She was sick for eight days. Later she told her friends what had happened: "I will always remember their faces, but I cannot hate them."

Teresa suffers as a result of her rape, but she also suffers because of the misery of her people. One day she left to join her people hiding in the mountains, taking with her the best that she had to offer — her faith in God and her nursing skills. Her life in the mountains was difficult, but she was accompanying her people in their passion and sorrow. At times she found herself praying to God as she crouched in a primitive shelter dug into the ground, watching the bombs fall.

"Life was hard. We had very little, but we still shared. I imagined Jesus and his disciples fleeing when the authorities persecuted them. They slept in the hills and shared what little they had with each other and with the poor."

Then in the midst of a bombing raid, a woman went into labor. Suddenly somebody cried out, warning the people to take cover. Teresa tried to help the woman, but they were unable to reach shelter. They took refuge beneath the shade of a tree, and there, amid the bombs and bullets, the child was born.

Teresa was afraid; her legs wanted to run back to the shelter, but she couldn't leave the mother. The bombing attack lasted an hour, and Teresa didn't have anything with which to cover the child. Today the mother and child are alive. Teresa says she thanks God for giving her the strength to stay and help the mother.[3]

In the midst of a tragic war, Teresa's story is a testimony of love. It is not a unique story, as so many of us who encountered this church of the poor during the war years can testify. Teresa exemplifies the grace of the poor that Romero experienced over and over. Yet such stories are not meant to romanticize war. The war hardened many hearts, divided families, embittered and dehumanized people. Justice and peace do not come easy. It is one of many hidden miracles that the war occasioned: that some, often those considered insignificant, could rescue love from the ballast of hatred that engulfed them. Thousands of people like Teresa, inspired by their faith in a God of life and encouraged by the pastoral example of Archbishop Romero, put a human face on tragedy. Her spirit, like Romero's, drew her to a deeper solidarity with the poor. In one of his homilies, Romero said:

> *My position as a pastor obliges me to be in solidarity with all who suffer, and to make every effort for the sake of people's dignity.*[4]

Teresa's testimony is an example of "the pastoral work of accompaniment" about which Romero spoke in his fourth pastoral letter. He defined it as *"personal evangelization of those Christian individuals or groups who have made a concrete political option which, according to their conscience, is their faith commitment in history."*[5] The seeds of such evangelization, however, were already present in the poor.

Ismael is another example of this pastoral accompaniment. In a letter to his parish priest, he describes his life as a lay catechist accompanying the people in a war zone: "Truly we have seen the presence of God," he writes. "Today I see clearly what the Scriptures say about the power and love of God for our people."

Ismael is one of hundreds of peasants, men and women, who carried out a pastoral ministry among the villages most affected by the war, accompanying the people as they fled from the army to the mountains for safety. It is difficult to imagine these assemblies. Huddled beneath an overcrop of bush or the camouflage of trees, a peasant church gathered beneath the stars, often anxious about lighting candles for fear of detection. There they celebrated the Word of God at night and reflected on the Gospel of another outcast. And their hope matched the imaginative hope of Jesus.

"Father," Ismael wrote to his pastor, "we suffer a great deal here. Our bodies are wasting away, and we have many worries. The old people and the children we have to carry concern all of us. We have no money, no clothing, no shoes. But God will look after us. We are going to suffer in this life. These are only the birth pangs, but joy will come. The consoling words of Christ will wipe away every tear. No more will there be crying, pain, worry, or death — everything will pass away. Our hope is to know God."[6]

This letter, in all of its simplicity, is a revealing testimony of the profound life of faith of the Salvadoran poor, of their thorough embrace of the Gospel and its consequences. It is the faith of the Christian communities in the midst of their passion, and the hope that they express for resurrection.

These stories of pastoral accompaniment express the great suffering endured by the poor of El Salvador during the most difficult moments of the war. But they also express the great love of the poor for one another. Archbishop Romero, reflecting on his ministry, once said:

> With people such as this, it's not difficult to be a Good Shepherd. These are people who impel to service those who have been called to defend their rights and to be their voice. So for me, even more than a service that has merited such generous praise, it is a duty that fills me with profound satisfaction.[7]

With each step Romero took closer to the people he discovered in himself a depth of spirit that no other spiritual discipline could touch. As he accompanied the people, he discovered on the path suffering that challenged his most fundamental understanding of life, of God. With Jeremiah he could say, "We look for peace, but find no good; for a time of healing but there is terror instead" (14:19). Romero would not, could not avoid that terror.

But each Sunday he could demonstrate publicly his practice of accompaniment by naming from the pulpit those who had been detained, disappeared, murdered. He also made clear over and over again his call to those who were torturers and murderers to hear God's Word and to be converted:

> *And so, brothers and sisters, I repeat what I have said here so often, addressing by radio those who perhaps have caused so many injustices and acts of violence, those who have brought tears to so many homes, those who have stained themselves with the blood of so many murders, those who have hands soiled with tortures, those who have calloused their consciences, who are unmoved to see under their boots a person abased, suffering, perhaps ready to die. To all of them I say: No matter your crimes. They are ugly and horrible... but God calls you and forgives you.*[8]

Like Jeremiah, the poor lived in what the poet José Martí called "the hour of the furnaces." Death triumphed, "cutting down the children in the street, young people in the squares, the corpses of the slain like dung on a field, like sheaves behind the harvester, with no one to harvest them" (Jer. 9:20–21).

Two more stories from *Letter to the Churches* provide a glimpse at the life-and-death struggle of the poor during the years of war and how they became protagonists in their resistance to the forces of death. Jacinta, an elderly peasant woman who lived in a poor neighborhood at the edge of San Salvador, recalled the terror of that time: "When night comes, I wish I were a dove so I could fly away and not have to be home during these hours."

One night, six men from the death squads came to her shack looking for guns. When they didn't find anything, they upset the sacks filled with corn shucks the family used to light their home during the long nights. They pointed their guns at Jacinta and told her not to move. Then they knocked her husband down in front of her, stepped on him and kicked him, breaking his neck.

"God sees what you do," Jacinta told them, "and God will make you pay for this shameful act."

"God is dead!" one of the men shouted. "We are the gods now."

They dragged her two oldest daughters outside. Three men beat them, and then they raped each one. When they finished, Jacinta was forced to serve them water at gunpoint.

"Don't tell anyone about this. If you do, we're going to come at night and kill everyone."

The youngest daughter, who was five years old at the time, witnessed everything that happened. Since then, she hardly speaks; she only cries. Jacinta's two daughters were left pregnant; her husband is unable to do anything; and Jacinta is terrified.[9]

Such scenes were repeated nightly in hundreds of humble dwellings throughout El Salvador prior to the war. For three of those years, Archbishop Romero never ceased to confront the new "gods." Romero and the church of the poor struggled to hold open the one space the security forces could not obliterate with their M-16s, their bombs, and their torture chambers — the space of witness. If the church of the poor could not prevent life from being taken, they could bear witness to the sacredness of life, even as the state demanded absolute obedience. Romero was unable to protect the people. His command to the army to cease the repression failed. Where he didn't fail, however, and where his people did not falter, is in the realm of fidelity to the Gospel. Jacinta was right: God was still present, even as her daughters were dragged away and raped, even as her husband's neck was broken. The gods of death could not kill the God of life. As long as the people held firm, like Job, to their faith in God, even in the midst of their torment and crucifixion, the powerful could claim no triumph. No human logic could make sense of the horrors they endured. Evil cannot be explained, only resisted. But a Gospel for outcasts subverted the world's logic. Outcasts were, and are, the face of God in history.

This is the commitment of being a Christian: to follow Christ in his incarnation. If Christ, the God of majesty, became a lowly human and lived with the poor and even died on a cross like a slave, our Christian faith should also be lived in the same way. The Christian who does not want to live this commitment of solidarity with the poor is not worthy to be called Christian.[10]

What spirituality, then, animated the base Christian communities and was embodied by those who accompanied them? How did they keep faith and encourage each other? How did the people accompany the poor? How did their spirituality affect Romero and impact the church of El Salvador?

Salvadoran peasants and workers do not speak of "spirituality." Spirituality is for clerics, not for the poor. The Salvadoran poor would hardly see themselves as spiritual teachers. But if they were to speak of the "spirituality" that enlightened their passion for justice, they would speak of *mística*. *Mística* points to the invisible bond that unites people to each other — the bond of one-heartedness that allows us to call each other brother and sister. *Mística* is the spirit of community. It transcends any one individual yet is immanent in the relational world. The *mística* of the liberation process, revealed in community, is what the poor offer as a sign of God's presence. *Mística* calls forth the prophetic, the depths of communal prayer, and a sense of the needs of all that transforms and purifies self-interest. *Mística* makes it possible for a community to risk itself so that others might live. It is closely linked to *entrega*, the ability to give yourself to the cause of the poor.

This dimension of the liberation process was evident in the reflections of a base Christian community from Morazán that used the illumination of the flaming *ocote* branch to describe their spirituality. Here is their reflection on the spirituality, the *mística*, that animated their lives:

> Someone blows a few times on the coals that seemed dead and they begin to glow and the puff of breath brings the flame to the *ocote*. That's what happened in our lives. The breath came, and the wind brought us the light that broke the night. And our communities became a living church. The word of God came to us and poor people began to have faith in other poor people.... This book is subversive

because it turns the tortilla over, because it throws down the order of kings and empires and it puts the poor on top.... Our finding the Bible was like an earthquake.

After that, Archbishop Romero arrived, who preached the word of God in the midst of repression. His prophetic voice fanned the *ocote*. The red coals became fire. It was he who did this.... We began to see the Christian faith was also a task and obligation. And that is how we poor men and women began to stop believing in the false promises of outsiders, the great and powerful, and we turned to our neighbors to reflect with them, to organize with them, to believe with them.... Believing in God, and believing in our brothers and sisters, we began our journey.[11]

Mística has everything to do with history. In this sense the spirituality of the poor subverts our notions of a contemplative spirituality that is individualistic, that is the purview of the knowledgeable, the "advanced," the monk. *Mística* reveals the extraordinary in the ordinary events of history. *Mística* requires not so much an individual listening to the voice of God within, but an attention to the voice of God revealed in the cries and whispers of the poor in our midst. Salvadoran peasants and workers knew that a time would come when they would face the torturers, a time of stark aloneness. The poor of El Salvador knew the dark night of the soul intimately. They understood that they risked standing, figuratively and literally, naked, alone before God. Daily they lived the stages of the traditional spiritual path of purgation, illumination, and contemplative unity. They experienced purgation not only in their flesh during torture, but in the depths of their souls when they cried out over and over again at the ignominy they suffered and the world turned away; still they clung to God. In turn the Word of God illuminated their struggle, and the bond of community provided a profound sense of communion, especially when penetrated by the spirit of the martyrs.

Mística is less about the ascent to a Mt. Carmel that is lofty and far from the people than it is about an immersion in the ordinary tasks that hold together life and hope and love. This *mística* is what transformed Romero. The heart of the world and the heart of the church of Christ is a mystery not contained by edifice or canon.

> *God saves in history. Each person's life, each one's history is the meeting place God comes to. How satisfying to know one need not go to the desert to meet him, need not go to some particular spot in the world. God is in your own heart.*[12]

Romero was not scandalized by the poor or by the cross they had to carry. And, because of his faithfulness, the poor were not scandalized by the church.

> *The subsecretary of the Ministry of Defense...told me... that they are offering me whatever protection I want, even a bulletproof car. I thanked him...saying respectfully that I cannot accept this protection since I want to run the same risks as the people do: that it would be an antipastoral witness were I to ride in such safety while my people are so insecure. I took the opportunity to ask him, rather, to protect the people in certain zones where the checkpoints, the military operations, do so much damage — or at least create so much terror.*[13]

When farmworkers, union organizers, or members of the Christian base communities in El Salvador gather to commemorate the heroism of their people, they enact a liturgy of memory that has profound creative power. The names of those who were killed in the service of liberation are called out, and after each name the community exuberantly shouts, *¡Presente!* The dead are truly present in that community. They are present, not simply by virtue of their claim that life is more than self-fulfillment; they are present in that space where life is held sacred. This holding of life as sacred, as imbued with *mística,* is not rhetorical but a daily creative task. In a culture of death, whether death by torture, poverty, or cynicism and despair, the task of keeping open the space for *mística* — for life itself and the hope for life —

belongs to those whose power derives from their spirit of resistance. The dead commemorated are those whose sense of life was countercultural, subversive, and imaginative.

What the Salvadoran dead resisted was death, the death of children ill from curable diseases, the death of hope in young people, the death of those who stood up to the gods of death, the death of the spirit when young women prostitute themselves to feed children or young men steal from the neighborhood poor. Death continues, and a spirit of irrepressible resistance continues as well. Resistance to death is impelled by memory. Not only do the people resurrect their dead through re-membering; the dead also resurrect the living.

> *Let us not think that our dead have gone away from us. Their heaven, their eternal reward makes them perfect in love: they keep on loving the same causes for which they died. Thus in El Salvador the force of liberation involves not only those who remain alive, but also those whom others have tried to kill and who are more present than before in the people's movement.*[14]

The evocation of memory is a creative act. The lives presented reestablish claims of justice and love as an immediate and inescapable invitation. The spirit of the martyrs has the audacious power to refuse death.

Every year, on the anniversaries of the deaths of the martyrs, the poor in El Salvador gather to commemorate the fallen. The witness of martyrs lives on and their memory inspires a rededication of one's life to the cause of justice for which they gave their lives. The devotion of the poor to the memory of the dead is especially poignant on All Souls' Day, November 2, the day to remember their loved ones with gratitude.

But for thousands of families who have not been able to fulfill the sacred obligation of burying their dead this day has a special sadness. They don't know what happened to their loved ones who were violently disappeared, tortured, and eliminated by the death squads. For these families, All Souls' Day is a day to weep silently as they recall the terrible scenes, knowing they cannot give their spouses, parents, or children a Christian burial. Yet often they have revealed to us the meaning of the word "forgiveness."

In one of the refugee camps during the war, hundreds of people, many of them children, had crowded around a table converted into an altar for Eucharist, singing: "We are a people on pilgrimage." Before the offertory, two children and four adults approached the altar with six posters; five of the posters were decorated with flowers, crowns, and hearts and carried the names of their dead relatives or of the priests and nuns killed during the war. The sixth poster had no flowers, but only the words: "May God forgive our enemies who have died." An elderly man explained the meaning of this poster:

> We made these posters instead of placing flowers on the graves of our dead. We all wrote the names of our dead relatives. But we are Christians, and we believe the names of our enemies should be placed on the altar, too, though without flowers. They are our brothers and sisters, even though they kill us. It's easy to love our own, but God asks us to love those who persecute us as well.[15]

The spirit of Salvadoran martyrs is a profound presence in history and at the heart of *mística*. Romero's memory is a central part of the *mística*. There is no litany of the fallen in El Salvador that does not include the people's shout of *¡Presente!* when the name of Oscar Romero is called out. That a martyred Romero's name would be invoked in this way is not a surprise. The presentation of the dead is, tragically, a tradition in Central America. But Romero made a bolder claim about himself. He said his spirit would be resurrected among the Salvadoran people. This was God's surprise in history.

How was it possible for Oscar Romero to have made such an audacious claim to a journalist shortly before his death? Such a claim is either the posture of a leader with an inflated ego or a person so deeply identified with those he loves that he can assume their faithfulness not simply to his memory but to the ineffable Spirit that has called them to a path that was, and is, both doomed and luminous. Romero's faith in the people's rejection of idols and their trust in the God of life reached beyond El Salvador's war, beyond his life, beyond the Peace Accords that would be signed twelve years after his death. Romero sought a peace with justice, a time when mothers would not have to carry small coffins to cemeteries because they could not afford the Pepto-Bismol that could save a dysentery-dehydrated infant from death. *"Peace,"* he said, *"is not the silence of cemeteries."*[16]

In a homily given just eight days before his death, Archbishop Romero spoke of the sacredness of life, especially the lives of outcasts:

> *Nothing is as important to the church as human life, the human person, especially the lives of the poor and the oppressed...Jesus said that whatever is done to the poor is done to him. This bloodshed, these deaths, are beyond all politics. They touch the very heart of God.*[17]

Romero's spirituality clearly was rooted in the space where life itself is sacred, vulnerable, threatened by death — and for that very reason is precious.

The Mothers of the Disappeared bore witness to the meaning of life and death by refusing to allow the Salvadoran government to forget the lives of the dead and disappeared. In addition to the seventy-five thousand who were killed during the war, many others were detained or vanished. Some were later found in jails; others had fled; but seven thousand were "disappeared" by the death squads, their bodies dumped in such infamous places as El Playón and La Puerta del Diablo, where vultures fed on the decaying cadavers.

When the Mothers of the Disappeared came to Romero for help, he encouraged them to form their own organization, both as a consolation to other mothers and as a refusal to let their children or spouses, who had been disappeared, become anonymous. Romero said:

> *No one can understand as well as a mother the value of the person, especially when this person is her own child. Why*

did they torture him? Why did they make her disappear?
The presence of a mother who weeps for the disappeared is
a presence that denounces; it is a presence that cries out to
heaven for the appearance of her disappeared child.... This
is the voice of justice, this is the voice of love, this is the cry
that the church gathers up from so many abandoned homes
to say, "This should not be!"[18]

Organized as the Mothers of the Disappeared, they were
courageous and prophetic. They refused to let their beloved son,
daughter, or husband "disappear." In so doing, they took from
the state its power to define the dead or imprisoned as anonymous, as terrorists, or as subversives. The mothers marched
through the streets of San Salvador, bearing the photos of their
beloved family members and demanding to know their where-
abouts, refusing to allow a murderous state to have the last word
or to give false meaning to the lives or deaths of those who
had been detained and disappeared. Mothers, as the bearers of
life, confronted those who took life. In the midst of tragedy, the
mothers resacralized the broken bodies of their family members.
They opened a space for memory, not only of death and torture,
but also of love, and this memory shaped their resistance to the
authors of death.

Romero sought a dynamic peace that addressed the need for
concrete historical solutions to people's desperate needs. He did
not foresee the outcome of the war that would reproduce conditions of servitude more violent than the conditions that sparked
the irruption of the poor; nor did he see the economic enslave-
ment whereby the people or the nation's economy would be
dependent on international creditors. What he did see was his
people's spirit. What he staked his life on was a Word so creative
that it challenged and overcame death itself.

Romero's spirituality revealed itself fully when the price of fidelity became his very life. In such a dynamic tension between life
and death, commitment is utterly clarified, lucid. Brazilian educa-
tor Paulo Freire said: "Life is risk. If I do not risk, I cannot be."
Those who risk much for the sake of justice become more and

more alive even if life is taken from them. The spirit of Oscar Romero, who was vivaciously, luminously alive, is living memory. Memory carries the dynamic invitation to risk oneself for the sake of justice for all, a vision of love that refuses inequality or any privilege. Romero discovered the memory of Jesus' spirit among outcasts and "subversives." It allowed him to transform his life. His prophetic courage was rooted in the spirit of the poor who followed an itinerant rabbi, defender of peasants and denouncer of idols, who was crucified on a cross as a blasphemer and rebel and raised by God to new life.

As a Christian, Romero believed in Jesus' resurrection from the dead. But as the shepherd of the archdiocese, he would come to believe in the resurrection of his people and even in his own resurrection. He was clear: he did not believe in death without life. In fact, he no longer believed in death. His spirituality was transformed as he experienced the people's continual rejection of death and resistance to intimidation.

> *"God's reign is already present on our earth in mystery. When the Lord comes, it will be brought to perfection"* (Gaudium et Spes, 39). *That is the hope that inspires Christians. We know that every effort to better society, especially when injustice and sin are so ingrained, is an effort that God blesses, that God wants, that God demands of us.*[19]

This resistance flew in the face of ordinary experience, of what one might expect of a people journeying through hell. The Salvadoran poor loved life, but they loved each other more, and so they rejected the state's weapon — death itself. Inspired by catechists who died defending the lives of community members or pastoral workers who became targets because they denounced the army's pacification programs of intimidation and terror, Romero no longer believed that death could kill this spirit. He became a prophet because of his people's prophetic choice: we are more than our deaths; our spirit of life transcends us all. Death no longer took his breath away, even as the army continued its awful mutilations, skinning alive popular leaders, slashing throats, and incinerating babies. Oscar Romero became more and more serene in his denunciations as death approached, surrounding him, hounding him, demanding despair or paralyzing horror.

"History will not perish," Romero said, *"because God sustains it."* None of the particular histories of those killed would perish because the reign of God, incarnate in those particularities, does not perish. Death as the final instrument of abusive power dies in the presence of the brazen dead and the living who resist and remember.

With a few other religious leaders in the twentieth century — like Martin Luther King, Jr., and Mahatma Gandhi — Romero was cast into the realm of historical struggle. Yet he navigated a simultaneously historical and transcendent path, often misunderstood by both enemies and friends. He believed in history as the site of God's presence. But he also believed that:

> *There is something beyond history. There is something that moves the threshold of matter and time. There is something called the transcendent, the eschatological, the beyond, the final goal. God . . . is the final goal to which the risen Christ calls us.*[20]

The fact that Romero was misunderstood by enemies was not the source of his sorrow as much as it was a source of his apprehension. What hurt was the way in which he was misunderstood by his fellow bishops who, with the exception of Bishop Rivera y Damas, criticized his theology as too historically imbedded and insufficiently attendant to the transcendent. The spirituality of the other Salvadoran bishops was at best based on a theology of transcendence that insulated them from the people's crucifixion, keeping their religious faith "pure" and unsullied by history and, at worst, openly allied with the interests of the wealthy and powerful. A year before Romero was killed, they not only "reported" Romero to the nuncio; they sent a secret document to the Holy See. At that time, Romero wrote in his diary:

> *They denounce me to the Holy See in matters of faith, say I am politicized, accuse me of promoting a pastoral work with erroneous theological grounding — a whole se-*

*ries of accusations that completely impugn my ministry as a
bishop. In spite of how serious this is, I feel great peace. I
acknowledge my deficiencies before God, but I believe that
I have worked with goodwill and that I am not guilty of the
serious things of which they accuse me. God will have the
last word on this.*[21]

The powerful knew, too, that Romero did not have much
support from Rome. The only true encouragement he received
came early on from Pope Paul VI who took his hands and said,
"Courage, brother, courage!" He also received support from
his one curia friend, Cardinal Eduardo Pironio, prefect of the
Congregation of Religious:

*The pope made us sit one on each side of him and, address-
ing himself to me in particular, he took my right hand and
kept it between his two hands. I would have liked to have
had a photograph of that moment, which expressed such
intimate communion between a bishop and the center of
Catholic unity. And holding my hands that way, he talked
to me for a long time.*

*It would be difficult for me to repeat his long message
exactly because, besides being more detailed than I expected, and rather cordial, ample, generous — because of
the emotion of the moment — I cannot remember it word
for word. But the principal ideas of his words were these:
"I understand your difficult work. It is work that can be
misunderstood; it requires a great deal of patience and a
great deal of strength. I already know that not everyone
thinks like you do, that it is difficult in the circumstances
of your country to have this unanimity of thinking. Nevertheless, proceed with courage, with patience, with strength,
with hope."*[22]

The Salvadoran bishops' criticism of Romero was also made
public in El Salvador. Romero describes a diocesan senate meeting in which they learn that Bishop Alvarez read a document to
a meeting of the clergy of his diocese in San Miguel *"that de-*

nounces the attitude of the archbishop and the archdiocese. I told the diocesan clergy that, as far as I was concerned, we should use this criticism as an opportunity to review our actions sincerely and with humility."[23]

Romero repeatedly answered their charges, always seeking reconciliation without loss of integrity. Romero wrote in his diary that he agreed with the nuncio that he should cooperate and give in, *"but not in substance, not when it has to do with being true to the Gospel, to the teaching of the church and especially to this suffering people who would find it hard to understand this."*[24]

Twelve days before his death, on the anniversary of the death of Father Rutilio Grande, Romero had to meet with the other bishops of El Salvador in Ayagualo at Rome's request. The nuncio from Costa Rica arrived to broker an election of the president and vice-president of the Bishops Conference, as well as to promote unity among the bishops. Traditionally, the archbishop of San Salvador was elected president, but this time the four other bishops blocked this option and even reneged on their promise to elect Bishop Rivera y Damas as the vice-president. Instead, they elected Bishop Eduardo Alvarez president, canceled their previous vote for Rivera y Damas on some arcane procedural grounds, and elected Bishop Pedro Aparicio as vice-president. Romero called the meeting "very fruitful." Nevertheless, he wrote in his diary:

> *I fear, given the aggressiveness with which Bishop Aparicio and Bishop Alvarez attacked me, that we have not achieved much with respect to deep feelings of unity. The Lord will judge. On my part, I want to offer up all these sacrifices and all this unpleasantness so that the Gospel may triumph and so that we all may be converted to the truth and to the service of God and our people.*[25]

Though he was deeply hurt by the bishops' rejection of him at the beginning of his ministry, Romero was beyond their criticism by the time of that Bishops Conference election. James Brockman describes him as sitting through meetings with the bishops virtually in silence while they carped about this or that complaint with his diocese, especially his using the seminary as a refuge center for the hundreds of peasants pouring into the city in flight from bombardment and search-and-destroy patrols in the rural areas.

As if the bishops' criticisms were not enough, Romero was also pressed by some of the popular organizations and guerrilla groups to take more forceful stands. Although he was courageous in defending the people's right to organize, calling the popular organizations *"the signs of God's presence and purposes,"* he also challenged them. He was surefooted in making his claim for nonviolence and in discerning God's presence in the people's struggles. When militants of the popular organizations or guerrilla groups occupied the cathedral, however, he was not willing to forcibly evict them simply because they claimed the church as theirs in the cause of the people and refused to leave. But Romero was on solid ground in admonishing the organizations that they could not speak exclusively for the people nor ignore their hunger, not just for bread, but for God. For example, when one of the guerrilla groups occupied the cathedral and a church in the center of San Salvador, Romero met with their leaders to ask them to allow the church to be used again for Mass and worship. He told them that *"respect for the Christian sentiments of the majority of the people would be a necessary condition for them to have the popularity they lack now when they are attacking these feelings."*[26]

What was more complex and troubling for Romero than challenges from the government, the left, or even the other bishops was being pushed by his own priests to positions he didn't feel he could take. Two priests nudged Romero to accept the leadership of the popular organizations that were working with people in the refugee centers that the diocese staffed and co-administered with the people. Romero, however, was adamant that the centers should not be used to recruit or proselytize the refugees.

To all of his critics Romero was forgiving. The misunderstandings for him were not so much personal or even ideological as spiritual:

Those who do not understand transcendence cannot understand us. When we speak of injustice here below and

*denounce it, they think we are playing politics. It is in the
name of God's just reign that we denounce the injustices of
the earth.*[27]

For Romero God is not distant: *"Transcendent, yes, infinite,
but a God close at hand here on earth."*[28] God is nearest those
who are empty. Few understood Romero's genuine humility. As
a seminarian and young priest he was, like his friend Rutilio
Grande, scrupulous and self-effacing. As archbishop he would
grow to a courage and a certainty that would allow him to
challenge church and state. But he still experienced himself as a
wounded healer, someone who had a great deal to learn from the
poor. The essence of his own mystical personality is that he was
not self-sufficient. He needed God and he needed the people to be
grounded, to know which way to turn:

> *The person who feels the emptiness of hunger for God is
> the opposite of the self-sufficient person. In this sense rich
> means the proud, rich even means the poor who have no
> property but who think they need nothing, not even God.*[29]

Romero's life and death bore witness to the claim that commitment to the poor is the way we discover the sacred. What basis is
there to this claim? Why do the Salvadoran poor, or the poor of
Guatemala or Nicaragua or southern Mexico, reveal God's reign
in a preeminent and imaginative way? Is this claim simply ro-
mantic or apologetic? Martyred Jesuit Ignacio Ellacuría claimed
that "with Archbishop Romero God had visited El Salvador."
Was this assertion metaphoric or a statement of experience? Revelation breaks forth from the marginalized and poor precisely in
such experiences of life and death.

James Alison, in *Raising Abel: The Recovery of the Eschatological Imagination,* wrote:

> The coming into existence of the kingdom incorporates
> a whole lot of people of no importance, of no apparent
> worth.... Only that which is vulnerable can allow itself to
> be broken in order to be built up again.[30]

Those without power unmask the structures that protect the powerful. Those who are crushed begin an interrogation of the mighty. Those dispossessed of power see through its cosmetics. People in El Salvador refer to a person who listens more than he or she speaks as *humilde* — humble. What Romero experienced was a people, *los humildes*, who were listening for a Word that alone could make sense of their inexpressible pain. How little the poor demanded, how much hope they discovered in their own impossible situation.

What was their hope as the death tolls mounted, as they faced electric shock, as the mask filled with lye was placed over their heads? What was their hope after the FMLN's first offensive failed and the United States began sending more and more military aid? Again, Alison wrote:

> There is nothing pretty about Christian hope. Whatever Christian hope is, it begins in terror and utter disorientation in the face of the collapse in all that is familiar. . . . It is no longer hope of a rescue, but a fixed surety of that which is not seen, where there seems to be no way out, and where death and its system seem absolutely dominant; and it is this fixed surety of that which is not seen which empowers us to the forging of a counterhistory to that of the domination of death.[31]

Romero and his church of the poor faced death, but they still believed it had no hold. Quite simply, they did not hope in "the world" anymore — understood as the dominant world that excluded them. That world had betrayed them. They faced the depths of evil and saw death call them by name, and because they had no other choice, they chose a new path in history beyond death. Dying, they rose, most of them anonymously, unlike their beloved pastor. In El Salvador, those who were dead, or in the poet Roque Dalton's words "half-dead," rose up. The victims acquired a voice, and people revealed the face of the Gospel that Romero preached. In the struggle between death and life, the Word remains.

4

The Testimony of the Martyrs

In this situation of conflict and antagonism, in which just a few persons control economic and political power, the church has placed itself at the side of the poor and has undertaken their defense. The church cannot do otherwise. ...But by defending the poor, it has entered into serious conflict with the powerful, who belong to the monied oligarchies, and with the political and military authorities of the state. This defense of the poor in a world so deep in conflict has occasioned something new in the recent history of our church: persecution.[1]

Reflecting on one of her last interviews with Archbishop Romero, human rights worker and writer Carolyn Forche remembers watching him walk beneath the bougainvillea and fire trees in the garden adjoining his small room in the Divina Providencia hospital. Tensions were rising — in only ten days he would be assassinated — but Romero made himself available, demonstrating his calm demeanor and remarkable trust in his people. Carolyn described how vulnerable he was; only days before a cache of dynamite set to blow up during his Mass at the basilica had been discovered. "I noticed a luminosity about him that I had not seen issue from anyone else. He is holy," I thought. "He is already a saint."[2]

Oscar Romero is not holy simply because of the way he died, but because of the way he lived. His martyrdom was only a final sign, a confirmation of his holiness. Like the other signs — ac-

companiment of the poor, the Gospel proclaimed as good news
to the poor, and a faith that defends the life of the poor in the
midst of history's conflicts — his witness as martyr was intimately
linked to the poor. Romero wrote:

> *I rejoice in the fact that our church is persecuted, precisely*
> *for its preferential option for the poor, and for trying to in-*
> *carnate itself in the interest of the poor. And I want to say*
> *to our people, to the government officials, to the rich and*
> *powerful: If you don't become poor, if you don't become*
> *concerned for the poverty of our people, as you would for*
> *your own family, you will not be able to save our society.*[3]

Martyrdom, Romero believed, was a sign of fidelity. This is the
message that he proclaimed at the funeral Mass of Father Rafael
Palacios, the fourth priest killed in his archdiocese:

> *How sad it would be, in a country where such horrible mur-*
> *ders are being committed, if there were no priests among*
> *the victims! They are the testimony of a church incarnated*
> *in the problems of its people. . . . I am proud to be able to*
> *say that the Archdiocese of San Salvador does not want to*
> *be indifferent or in complicity with the situation of sin and*
> *structural violence that exists in our country.*[4]

Persecution results in martyrdom, but not in silencing the
church. *"This is what the feasts of our church are like,"* Romero
said at Rafael Palacios's funeral Mass, *"the blood of martyrdom*
and the hope of Christianity." And martyrdom brings credibility
to the church:

> *It is the glory of our church to have mixed its blood — the*
> *blood of its priests, catechists, and communities — with the*
> *massacres of the people, and ever to have borne the mark*
> *of persecution.*[5]

Each time he recalled the martyrdom of Rutilio Grande, Alfonso Navarro, Octavio Ortiz, Rafael Palacios, Ernesto Barrera,
and Alirio Napoleón Macías — the six priests killed in El Sal-

vador during Romero's lifetime — Romero saw the vulnerability of the poor:

> *If all this has happened to persons who are the most evident representatives of the church, you can guess what has happened to ordinary Christians, to the* campesinos, *catechists, lay ministers, and to the ecclesial base communities. There have been threats, arrests, tortures, murders, numbering in the hundreds and thousands. As always, even in persecution, it has been the poor among the Christians who have suffered most.*[6]

Romero did not meet death "with his arms folded," which is the metaphor Salvadorans use to describe a passive onlooker. He met death "open-armed" and engaged. He asked of death what he asked of life: *"liberation for my people and a testimony of hope for the future."* Such a death he would embrace, and his irrepressible homilies led him in that direction.

> *As a pastor, I am obligated by divine commandment to give my life for those I love... even for those who would assassinate me.... For that reason I offer God my blood for the redemption and resurrection of El Salvador.... Martyrdom is a grace that I don't believe I merit. But if God accepts the sacrifice of my life, may my blood be the seed of liberty and sign that this hope will soon become a reality. May my death, if it is accepted by God, be for the liberation of my people and a testimony of hope in the future.*[7]

While he was archbishop, Romero reminded the world that the privileged place of the church is among those who suffer, wherever they may be. Romero never promised the poor what he could not give — safety or an end to their impoverishment. He did not promise that the assassinations would end or that the pope would intervene on their behalf or that he could convince the president of the United States to stop aid to the Salvadoran military. He did not promise these things because he could not. What he promised was that he would accompany them through death and join them in meeting death if that was the price of his fidelity to them. He promised them that God would never abandon them — that is the good news of God that Romero proclaimed. No matter that his voice might be silenced, God's promise would not disappear:

> *Courage, dear friends. I know that for many the hour of testing has come, and they have fled as cowards: catechists, celebrants of the Word, people who shared with us the joys of our meetings, have been frightened. People we thought very strong are frightened away because they have forgotten that this is a religion of life, and, as life, it must clash with the life that is not God's life but exists as the kingdom of darkness.*[8]

So many turned away, even priests withdrew. Romero himself would be killed. But his promise remained.

> *The Word remains. This is the great consolation of one who preaches. My voice will disappear, but my word — which is Christ — will remain in the hearts of those who have wanted to receive it.*[9]

The story of Graciela and Ramón is an example of the Word remaining. Graciela and her husband, Ramón, were farmworkers who harvested sugarcane. One year they participated in taking over a parcel of land belonging to the plantation where they were employed. They asked the landowner for a better salary and for better food for the workers and their children. The work was hard, they had lots of children, and they were hungry. Before the land takeover, they had tried other means of protest but without success. This time the plantation owners called in the National Guard, who violently dislodged the protesters. Two hundred farmworkers were machine-gunned to death.

Ramón was one of the people killed, leaving Graciela a widow with eight children, including an eight-day-old baby. After the massacre, people fled to the hills for safety. Graciela's three oldest children — two boys and a girl — decided to join the liberation struggle. The other five younger children accompanied their mother to a refugee camp in San Salvador. There, amid hundreds of other peasant families who had fled to the capital for safety, Graciela's baby learned to walk and to speak.

By the time her baby was eighteen months old, Graciela decided to take her five children and go back to her village, despite the danger. A few weeks after they arrived, the village was bombed and later attacked by the army. Many women, elderly, and children died. Shrapnel from a mortar killed Graciela's baby as she fled to save her children's lives: "I heard a great explosion; then I realized that my child had been sliced in half, right in my arms."

Graciela returned to the refugee camp with her four remaining small children: "I didn't know what to do. I went days without eating or sleeping. I prayed a novena to the Virgin Mary, and she consoled me. She gave me strength to live. I feel now that I am ready to give my life, and the lives of my children if necessary, for the liberation of our people. Yes, all of us will offer our lives."[10]

In the parable of the Good Shepherd, Jesus says: "No one can take my life from me; I myself offer it freely" (John 10:18). The same sentiment was expressed by a Salvadoran peasant, "Before, we died or were killed, and we didn't know why. Today, perhaps all of us are going to die, but we are clear that we die for the sake of our people."[11]

Romero was worthy of the trust the poor placed in him. If you ask them, "Why did Archbishop Romero die?" many will tell you: "Because he spoke the truth." Romero did not hesitate to speak truth to power, but he spoke it with compassion, always praying for the conversion of his enemies:

> *Let us not be afraid to be left alone if it's for the sake of truth. Let's be afraid to be demagogues, coveting people's sham flattery. If we don't tell them the truth, we commit the worst sin: betraying the truth and betraying the people.*[12]

What Romero gave the poor were promises kept: he would not, whatever the cost, betray them. And he would remain with them always. What the state was unable to kill — in spite of modern weaponry, high-tech radar, and sophisticated reconnaissance capacity (no other region in the world received as much military assistance from the United States in the 1980s, except the countries of the Middle East) — was the imagination of Romero and the church of the poor. As the hour of his own agony approached, Romero expressed with conviction his and the Salvadoran people's victory:

> *I have frequently been threatened with death. As a Christian, I do not believe in death without resurrection. If they kill me, I will be resurrected in the Salvadoran people.*[13]

Romero could make this bold claim because he knew that the poor would make the spirit of the Gospel incarnate in history. Indeed, as if they were God's hands, they have resurrected their beloved pastor. This is not a feat accomplished by theologians intending to immortalize a courageous bishop. Nor is Romero's resurrection in his people a devotional memory imbued with popular pietism or sentimentality. It is the fulfillment of a promise, Romero's and the people's. It is their act of faith and the grace of God.

Although two decades have passed since his murder, Romero is truly present in his people. One can travel to the remotest area of the countryside and find in little houses with dirt floors and no electricity a photo on the wall of Monseñor Romero and beneath it a tin of fresh wildflowers. Monseñor lives in the daily life of the people. He goes forward: Risen!

In the last three months of his life, Romero seemed to enter a time of deep surrender to a situation that was steeped in terror. Perhaps he had never been so heartbroken as he listened to the reports of massacres and saw corpses left by the side of the road to horrify and suppress resistance. His homilies became more passionate, more tender and unafraid. In the midst of so much death, of threats to his pastoral teams, to priests and catechists, and to himself, he grew more confident that God lived among the Salvadoran poor, suffering with them, refusing vengeance.

> *If it were not for this prayer and reflection with which I try to stay united with God, I would be no more than what St. Paul says: clanging metal.... Let us see that Christ is in*

the midst of our people's political movement. Let us not let Christ be absent from our history. That is what is most important at this moment of our nation's history: That Christ be God's glory and power, and that the scandal of the cross and of pain not make us flee from Christ and cast aside suffering. Instead, let us embrace it.[14]

Exhausted, beset by challenges from the bishops, demands of the popular organizations and the Farabundo Martí National Liberation Front (Frente Farabundo Martí de Liberación Nacional, FMLN), and daily criticism from the political right in the newspapers, he grew to more clearly understand what it meant to be a good shepherd. It meant to lay down your life for your people. It meant believing in the destiny of the people beyond even your own ability to protect them. That must have been his deepest surrender: to let go of his fear for the future, his fear for the people if he were killed. Still he trusted his people and his God:

If someday they take away the radio station from us, if they close down the newspaper, if they don't let us speak, if they kill all the priests and the bishop too, and you are left a people without priests, each one of you must become God's microphone, each one of you must become a messenger, a prophet.[15]

During those final months, Romero met with an incredible array of people, many of whom came, like Nicodemus in the Gospel, under the cover of darkness to speak with him privately. These included officials of the Salvadoran government and members of the popular organizations; military officers and militants of revolutionary groups; the U.S. ambassador and the papal nuncio. They also included the poor, refugees fleeing the military repression in the rural areas, and mothers whose loved ones had been disappeared by the death squads.

As the violence escalated, Romero's homilies grew more intense, more direct, more deeply connected to those in grief, in terror. His denunciation of torture, disappearances, and assassinations occurred with greater frequency now, as the number of deaths reached more than a thousand each month. Those close to Romero attest to the fact that he became a transformed person as he proclaimed the Gospel from the pulpit to an overflowing crowd each Sunday.

> *During Mass...I received a warm reception after my trip. I felt a special affection in that church, which was very full; the crowd continued to swell as the Mass progressed. The homily went on for almost two hours. I think I may be going on too long, but I feel, even so, the need to guide these people who are listening to me avidly.*[16]

In those final three months, his homilies bear witness to an even deeper trust in the abiding presence of God in the suffering and struggles of his people:

> *Today I celebrated the Epiphany Mass in the cathedral. In my homily I compared this moment in El Salvador with the turbulence that the Gospel speaks of in Jerusalem when the three wise men were looking for the King. I said that we are looking with the same spirit for the salvation of our people, which God surely holds, for Epiphany shows us that God came for the salvation of all peoples.*[17]

In that same Epiphany homily, Romero reaffirmed his faith in the transcendent dimension of the liberation of his people:

> *I want to reaffirm my conviction, as a person of hope, that a new ray of salvation will come. I want to encourage those who have the good will to hear me. Nobody has the right to sink themselves in despair; all of us have the duty to search together for new paths and to actively hope as Christians.... What we must save above all is the liberation process of our people. The people have begun this process that has cost them so much blood, and it cannot be lost.*[18]

Two weeks later, at the anniversary of the death of Father Octavio Ortiz, he reminded the people gathered of the mission of the church:

I spoke in the homily of the two dimensions of our message of Christian liberation: the transcendent one, from which Octavio and the other dead speak to us, which is the goal and the destiny of our kingdom on earth; and the earthly one, the earth where we still have our feet planted, where we are to embody this transcendental message insofar as we work for the liberation of our people, for the Christian redemption of the world.[19]

The following week, after security forces had fired on a demonstration of the poor, Romero proclaimed:

The cry of liberation of our people is a cry that reaches up to God and nothing and nobody can detain it.... The great leader of our liberation is this Anointed One, the Lord who comes to announce the good news to the poor, to give liberty to the captives, to bear news of the disappeared, to bring joy to so many homes that are in mourning, so that a new society may appear as in the sabbatical year of Israel.... Christ has come precisely to announce the new society, the good news, the new times.[20]

The following Sunday, just seven weeks before his death, Romero traveled to the University of Louvain in Belgium to deliver the address on which we have meditated in these pages. When he returned, ten days later, he gave an encapsulated version of that address to an overflowing crowd in the Sacred Heart Basilica in San Salvador:

I talked about poverty, using the guidelines of the Medellín document, presenting it as a denunciation of the injustice of the world; as a spirit that is lived, relying on God; and as a commitment, that of Jesus Christ, who committed himself to the poor. The church also carries out the mission of Christ to call all people to salvation....

I illuminated the reality of the country with the light of the Beatitudes, read in today's Gospel, condemning the selfishness of the rich who insist on maintaining their privi-

leges, and giving direction, beginning from the needs of the poor, to the politics of our country.[21]

The next day, Romero received news that this homily had caused "a furor" in Rome:

Specifically, the letter to be sent to the president of the United States, which was read during the homily and which seems to be the principal motive for these comments, is inspired by the increasing danger that is represented by military aid to El Salvador.... My letter asks the president of the United States not to send military aid, because it would bring great injury to our people and the destruction of many lives.[22]

In fact, Romero had asked President Carter to stop sending all aid, including humanitarian aid, because, he said, it will be misused to *"repress our people."* Turning a deaf ear to Romero's plea, the U.S. Congress appropriated $5.7 million in military aid to El Salvador just one week after Romero's murder. The precedent was set. By the end of the twelve years of war, the United States was sending an average of $1 million a day to the Salvadoran government.

For weeks before Romero died, cadavers were piling up in the city's streets, the bodies marked with signs of torture. In one of his last homilies Romero grew more pointed in speaking out against the government:

My homily was inspired ... by God's message about personal conversion as an essential condition for salvation. I also referred, by application, to the two things that have been most obvious this week: the growing repression of the government against the people, especially against the popular organizations, and the agrarian reform and the nationalization of the banks.[23]

Romero condemned the government's policy as "reforms with repression." Increasingly, as the season of Lent approached, he discerned the passion, death, and resurrection of Christ as it was lived out by the Salvadoran people. As if he had reached a point of no return, when his vulnerable people were caught in the paws of a devouring animal, Romero rose like Daniel to meet the beast. But the military lion would not be tamed. No international help was forthcoming; the bishops, except for Bishop Rivera y Damas, had turned against Romero and the poor. Nothing stood between the people and a ravaging army whose target was not simply the guerrillas but the organized poor. Merely to attend Romero's Mass or even to listen to his homily on the radio was considered subversive. No one stood by the people except a church that believed in the Gospel and an archbishop who did not consider his own life to be more important than the lives of his people.

> *Those who... would save their lives (that is, those who want to get along, who don't want commitments, who don't want problems, who want to stay outside of a situation that demands the involvement of all of us) they will lose their lives. What a terrible thing to have lived quite comfortably, with no suffering... quite tranquil, quite settled, with good connections.... To what good?*[24]

On March 23, 1980, the fifth Sunday of Lent, Oscar Romero preached his last Sunday homily. He must have known the effect of his words. Prophetic, as always, and with absolute authenticity, he begged the military to stop killing their brothers and sisters. Then raising his voice to thunderous applause, he commanded them: *"Stop the repression!"*

More poignant than ever before in his call for peace, he addressed the military directly:

> *Brothers, you are from the same people; you kill your brother peasants.... No soldier is obliged to obey an order that is contrary to the will of God. Now it is time for you to recover your consciences so that you first obey conscience rather than a sinful order.... In the name of God, then, in the name of this suffering people, whose cries rise to the heavens, every day more tumultuously, I ask you, I beg, I order you in the name of God: stop the repression.*[25]

Theories about Romero's assassins abound. Most accuse Major Roberto D'Aubuisson, the founder of the ARENA Party, president of El Salvador's National Assembly in 1982, and principal architect of the death squads, of orchestrating Romero's murder. Others point to a civilian-military pact of wealthy landowners (most living in Miami mansions safe from the war's toll) and military commanders fearful that a deflated or mutinous army would not hold the line on land control. Most Salvadorans insist that no such assassination order could have been given without approval from the Military High Command. But nothing has ever been proven. Three days after Romero's assassination the judge assigned to the case, Atilio Ramírez Amaya, was shot at by two armed men. Ramírez Amaya escaped and left the country within days. Some eyewitnesses to Romero's assassination, including Napoleón Martínez, were disappeared; others fled the country. According to the U.N. Truth Commission, the assassination of Romero was orchestrated by Major Roberto D'Aubuisson.

It is pure speculation to imagine what Romero's killers said to each other after they received reports of his famous last homily addressed to the military. One might have expected some sophistication in their planning. But there was none. What might those conversations have been like? Perhaps some said, "Let's kill him right now, tonight, or tomorrow morning at the latest." Others might have countered, "No, it will be too obvious, immediately after his homily directed at the army." But the agitated won the argument — they would kill him the next day.

Were they aware of the potential symbolism? Did someone say, "Don't kill him at Mass, whatever you do. Don't shoot him then. You'll just create a martyr"? Apparently not. Instructions were simply given to kill Romero at the altar where he would be, as he was each day, unprotected. Their message was urgent: Romero's command, *"In God's name, stop the killing,"* was to be canceled. Once and for all, eliminate him. But what a liturgy they orchestrated, those high priests of evil who unconsciously moved their petty place in history to its most dramatic unfolding.

Shortly before his assassination in the chapel of the Divina Providencia hospital on March 24, 1980, Romero had told a journalist in an interview:

Martyrdom is a grace I don't believe I am worthy of. But if God accepts the sacrifice of my life, may my blood be a seed of liberty and the sign that hope will soon become a reality.[26]

The threats to his life had grown more frequent, and he had begun sleeping in a room behind the chapel. Four days before he was killed he named additional priest voters so that there would be a quorum to elect a successor in case of his death.[27]

He was warned not to offer the memorial Mass because it had, rather oddly, been announced in the newspapers. Nevertheless, he went ahead. The readings for that last Mass seem uniquely appropriate. He read Psalm 23: "The Lord is my Shepherd.... Though I walk in the valley of the shadow of death I fear no evil. You are at my side." The Gospel reading was John 12:23–26: "Unless the grain of wheat falls to earth and dies, it remains alone. But if it dies, it bears much fruit." In the brief homily that followed, Romero said:

You have just heard in Christ's Gospel that one must not love oneself so much as to avoid getting involved in the risks of life that history demands of us, and that those who fend off danger will lose their lives. But whoever out of love for Christ gives themselves to the service of others will live, like the grain of wheat that dies, but only apparently. If it did not die, it would remain alone.... Only in dying does it produce the harvest.[28]

Moments later a single shot pierced his heart as he prepared to lift up the gifts of bread and wine in the offertory of the Mass. Romero immediately slumped to the ground, blood pouring from his heart, his ears, his nose. His death symbolized the words of the great Salvadoran poet Roque Dalton, " ... that my veins don't end in me but in the unanimous blood of those who struggle for life, for love."[29] Here are the last words Oscar Romero spoke before a bullet shattered his heart:

> *Whoever offers their life out of love for Christ, and in ser-*
> *vice to others, will live like the seed that dies.... May this*
> *immolated body and this blood sacrificed for all nourish us*
> *so that we may offer our body and our blood as Christ did,*
> *and thus bring justice and peace to our people. Let us join*
> *together, then, in the faith and hope of this intimate moment*
> *of prayer....* [30]

As Oscar Romero fell, the sisters present at the Mass rushed to his aid. He was pronounced dead in the emergency room of a local hospital. One of the sisters described the moment of his death in great detail:

I was only ten feet away, sitting on the second pew on the east side, when Monseñor was shot. We were very atten-tive to the moment, as he had finished his homily. Then a shot rang out. It was a strange sound, perhaps because the microphone and the light were near by. It sounded like a bomb had exploded. He fell to the ground immediately.

It's strange, I didn't feel afraid. Instead, I felt courage and ran immediately to help Monseñor. But seeing the tremen-dous hemorrhage of blood flowing from his nose, mouth, and ears, and realizing I couldn't do anything, my first re-action was to look in the direction of the main door of the chapel from where the shot had been fired. I wanted to see who had done this, but I didn't see anybody.

At that point I realized that God had heard Monseñor's prayer. He always said that if such a thing were to occur, he hoped nobody else would be affected. The truth is, we all expected that this would happen one day; but we never imagined that anybody would dare commit such a sacrilege and kill him at the very moment he celebrated the Eucharist. If we look at it from the perspective of the people, perhaps it was better that way. Martyrdom is not granted to just any person, but only to those who are worthy of it. Monseñor was a saint, and his whole life was a great witness. So it was a crowning prize for him, especially since it happened at the altar.

It was as though the Lord had spoken to him: "I don't want you just to offer me bread. Now you are the victim, you are my offering." Monseñor fell immediately at the foot of the crucifix, offering up his priestly ministry just as he had done each day since his ordination. His enemies tried on countless occasions, just as they had tried to do with Jesus, to find a pretext to justify his death, but they never found anything bad about him.

We have to thank God, even though it is painful, because here in El Salvador we had a great prophet, a saint, who died at the altar and who intercedes now in heaven for the poor, for the peasants, for his flock. He died as Christ died. He said that he was afraid, and he knew what was going to happen to him; but he forgave those who were going to kill him, and he believed he would be resurrected in his people.

I think we already experience this resurrection. The faith of our people is growing, as is their hope that one day things will change. That's what Monseñor said in the last words of his homily: "If the grain of wheat does not die, it will bear no fruit; but if it dies, how great the fruit." He is like that grain of wheat that fell to the ground, bearing fruit in its time.[31]

"I think we already experienced this resurrection." Resurrection, yes, but also, tragically, more death, tragically more years of more death. Still, in the midst of it all, the Salvadoran poor continued to move forward with Romero in their hearts.

As well as anyone could be, Oscar Romero was ready to face his death. In his last retreat, made a few weeks before his death, he told his spiritual director:

> *My other fear is for my life. It is not easy to accept a violent death, which is very possible in these circumstances. . . . You have encouraged me, reminding me that my attitude should be to hand my life over to God regardless of the end*

> *to which that life might come; that unknown circumstances*
> *can be faced with God's grace; that God assisted the mar-*
> *tyrs, and that if it comes to this I shall feel God very close as*
> *I draw my last breath; but that more valiant than surrender*
> *in death is the surrender of one's whole life — a life lived*
> *for God.*[32]

To surrender one's whole life — a life lived for God. This sums up Romero's life and death. This was the basis of his serenity and joy, evident to a terrified people even in the midst of horror. He conveyed reassurance and hope by his authentic, deep confidence in God and by his spirit expressed in his actions or preaching. Romero became the Gospel he preached. Though quiet and reserved, he was a joyful man because the source of his joy was neither temperamental nor a posture for the sake of his frightened flock. His last Sunday homily is vintage Romero and a wonderful window into the spirituality of a man who embodied the very paschal joy that he proclaimed so boldly:

> *Easter is a shout of victory! No one can extinguish that life*
> *that Christ resurrected. Not even death and hatred against*
> *him and against his church will be able to overcome it. He*
> *is the victor! Just as he will flourish in an Easter of un-*
> *ending resurrection, so it is necessary to also accompany*
> *him in Lent, in a Holy Week that is cross, sacrifice, martyr-*
> *dom.... Happy are those who do not become offended by*
> *their cross!*
>
> *Lent, then, is a call to celebrate our redemption in that*
> *difficult complex of cross and victory. Our people are very*
> *qualified...to preach to us of the cross; but all who have*
> *Christian faith and hope know that behind this Calvary of*
> *El Salvador is our Easter, our resurrection, and that is the*
> *hope of the Christian people.*[33]

Cross and resurrection, death and life: these are the anchor points of Archbishop Romero's spirituality. And they are linked, not sequentially, as if the cross ultimately leads to resurrection. Rather, in the most cruel passion that his people were living, the

spirit of resurrection penetrated the darkness and offered light
and hope to the poor:

> *Today, as diverse historical projects emerge for our people,
> we can be sure that victory will be had by the one that
> best reflects the plan of God. And this is the mission of the
> church...to see how the plan of God is being reflected or
> disdained in our midst....*
>
> *That is why I ask the Lord during the week, as I gather
> the cry of the people, the aches of so much crime, and the
> ignominy of so much violence, that he give me the suit-
> able word to console, to denounce, to call for repentance;
> and even though I may continue to be a voice crying in the
> desert, I know that the church is making the effort to fulfill
> its mission.*[34]

Less remembered in his last homily is his deep insight into the
violence by which we are all implicated. Romero believed we
are holy because we are human; that our tolerance for violence
against each other was the great sin. He never lost sight of the
dignity of every person, who is a temple of the Holy Spirit:

> *How easy it is to denounce structural injustice, institu-
> tionalized violence, social sin! And it is true, this sin is
> everywhere, but where are the roots of this social sin? In
> the heart of every human being. Present-day society is a sort
> of anonymous world in which no one is willing to admit
> guilt, and everyone is responsible. We are all sinners, and we
> have all contributed to this massive crime and violence in
> our country. Salvation begins with the human person, with
> human dignity, with saving every person from sin. And in
> Lent this is God's call: Be converted!*[35]

Although Romero lifted up the unique dignity of each person,
he returned again and again to a spirituality that also sanctified
the social dignity of the community, the good of all. He said,
*"It is not just an individual conversion but a communal conver-
sion."*[36] God desires to save not only persons but entire peoples.
God's plan of salvation is to make the story of every people a

story of salvation. And the mission of the church is to illuminate the way:

> *Today El Salvador is living its own Exodus. Today we, too, are journeying to our liberation through the desert, where cadavers and anguished pain are devastating us, and where many suffer the temptation of those who were walking with Moses and who wanted to turn back.... God desires to save the people making a new history.... What is not repeated are the circumstances, the opportunities to which we are witnesses in El Salvador....*
>
> *History will not perish; God sustains it. That is why I say that in the measure that the historical projects attempt to reflect the eternal project that is God's, in that measure they are reflecting the reign of God, and this is the work of the church. Because of this, the church, the people of God in history, is not installed in any one social system, in any political organization, in any political party.... She is the eternal pilgrim of history and is indicating at every historical moment what reflects the reign of God and what does not. She is the servant of the reign of God.*[37]

Romero insists upon the transcendent dimension of liberation, what he calls the true or *definitive* liberation. Here, too, the logic of cross and resurrection applies. It is not by avoiding the demands of historical liberation that one reaches a definitive liberation, as though by avoiding the suffering of the cross one attains resurrection. It is precisely by incarnating our lives in the historical and conflictual struggles of our time — and especially those of the poor — that we discover God's plan and promise of salvation:

> *The true solution has to fit into the definitive plan of God. Every solution we seek — a better land distribution, a better administration and distribution of wealth in El Salvador, a political organization structured around the common good of Salvadorans — these must be sought always within the context of definitive liberation.... Without God, there can*

be no true concept of liberation. Temporary liberations, yes; but definitive, solid liberations — only people of faith can reach them. . . .

Do you see how life recovers all of its meaning? And suffering then becomes a communion with Christ, the Christ that suffers, and death is a communion with the death that redeemed the world? Who can feel worthless before this treasure that one finds in Christ, that gives meaning to sickness, to pain, to oppression, to torture, to marginalization? No one is conquered, no one; even though they put you under the boot of oppression and of repression, whoever believes in Christ knows that he is a victor and that the definitive victory will be that of truth and justice![38]

These three themes — the dignity of the human person and value of the most impoverished, the salvation of people in history, and the transcendent dimension of liberation witnessed in the lives of the martyrs — form the heart of Romero's spirituality. They can be found in almost every homily that he preached as archbishop of San Salvador. They led him inexorably to God and to the people of God, especially the poor. They exacted of him surrender, absolute surrender, to the demands of the Gospel in life and in death, and forgiveness of his enemies. Oscar Romero knew as well as anyone that to proclaim the Gospel in word and deed was to invite enemies to his doorstep. The remarkable thing, however, is that Romero, like Jesus, loved his enemies — he called them "brothers" even when he challenged them.

Like his friend Rutilio Grande, Romero died loving his enemies; and like the figure of the Bedouin in the desert — whose image he evoked in the funeral Mass of Alfonso Navarro — Romero died pointing the way to forgiveness and life: "Not there, but here." In the end, Romero forgave his assassins. In an interview with a journalist shortly before his death he said:

You can tell people, if they succeed in killing me, that I forgive and bless those who do it. Hopefully, they will realize that they are wasting their time. A bishop will die, but the church of God, which is the people, will never perish.[39]

On March 30, 1980, at Archbishop Romero's funeral Mass 150,000 people crowded into the square in front of the cathedral despite the risk of military assault. If they would kill the archbishop, who was safe? Predictably, nobody. As Cardinal Corripio of Mexico eulogized Romero, bombs exploded, sending those assembled into a panic. In the midst of pandemonium, Salvadoran soldiers positioned on rooftops around the plaza fired into the surging crowd desperately trying to enter the already packed cathedral. Dozens were crushed to death.

The military's "lesson" at that funeral Mass, written in the people's blood and burned into national consciousness, was that those who keep alive the spirit of Romero will also be eliminated. Thirty were killed that day, and another four hundred were injured. As sniper fire repeatedly burst from the surrounding rooftops, Archbishop Romero's coffin was pulled into the cathedral, where he was hurriedly buried. He was laid down, as he lived, in the embrace of the disposable poor.

The significance of the violence at Romero's funeral Mass was not lost on Gustavo Gutiérrez, who was there:

> It was a tragic Sunday, as many will surely remember, when thirty or forty people were killed.... Could Monseñor Romero, who wanted to give his life for his people, have been buried in a kind of oasis of peace? Many of us asked ourselves that question, almost discreetly, as we buried him two hours after being enclosed in the cathedral. Could he have been buried in isolation from the reality that his people lived daily? Unfortunately, it could not have been otherwise. Monseñor Romero's burial took place in the midst of the suffering and struggles of his people.[40]

The death of Archbishop Romero was an occasion for profound sorrow and, in time, for profound joy — the same sorrow and joy that Romero himself attributed to the commemorations of the martyrs over which he presided. In Gutiérrez's words:

> [Romero's] death, in spite of the immense impact of sorrow that it brought us... was also a source of joy, because one

could see in Monseñor Romero the integral witness of a Christian dedicated to announcing the Word, bearing witness to the reign of God, and offering solidarity to those who suffered injustice. The integrity of his life is an example of something extraordinary.[41]

Gutiérrez further characterized the life and death of Romero as a watershed in the history of the Latin American church: "I think that we could say, without exaggeration, that the life and death of Monseñor Romero divides the recent history of the Latin American church into a before and after."[42]

Like the martyrdoms that preceded Romero's, and those that came after, his death offers light and life to a church that has been, from its inception, a church of the martyrs and a church of the poor:

> The martyrdom of Monseñor Romero allows us to see with greater clarity the witness of many other martyrdoms — of peasants, lay people, religious, and priests in Latin America: martyrdoms that many people scandalously still do not accept. The death of Monseñor Romero illuminates the sacrifice of their lives, and the lives of all those who unfortunately have followed. Romero's death is one of those deaths that bear witness to life in a profound way, even to a church that, since its inception, has always lived and blossomed from the blood of the martyrs.[43]

The Exodus of the people of El Salvador continued throughout the years of the war. Like the children of Israel after they had fled from bondage in Egypt, the years in the wilderness were years of trial and testing. With St. Paul they could say: "They treat us as liars, although we speak the truth; they regard us as strangers, although we are well-known. We are half dead, but we continue to live; they punish us, but they have not killed us" (2 Cor. 6:8–9).

Toñita is a Salvadoran peasant woman who reflects this spirituality of martyrdom. Toñita fled with her family and five thousand others to the mountains in search of refuge when the army invaded her village. She scrambled down to the Sumpul

River, dropping baskets and other belongings along the way in a frantic attempt to cross the river before the soldiers caught up to them. Everybody fled; children ran downstream; those who were too weak to swim, like the elderly, drowned; those who could, somehow threw themselves into the river and were shot. Only a few crossed to safety.

At about six in the evening, they reached a small village and continued their flight, winding their way through ravines, hiding behind the underbrush, until they reached the top of a hill where they passed the night. There they stayed for two days. The children cried out in hunger; others died because there was nothing to eat and their mothers had no milk to nurse them. The cries of the children pierced the night air.

Sometimes, when the soldiers came near, mothers would stuff rags in their children's mouths so that they wouldn't cry; a few of the children suffocated. This continued for days; at night they fled from one ravine to another. Mothers were exhausted, and the children hardly cried anymore; they were dying of hunger and thirst.

Toñita recalled vividly this Salvadoran Exodus: "As we reached the top of a hill, the soldiers detected us. Helicopters began to encircle us. Bullets rained down on all sides. We fled in all directions, trying to escape. We all wept to see the dead. It's terrible to walk by and see a dead child here, or an old man shot there, and another further on. We went nine days without food. But by the power of God and the Holy Virgin, we survived."

In the midst of the war Toñita expressed what a loss it was for the people when Romero was assassinated: "I remember what the people of Israel lived through in the past, and that's exactly what we are living through today. How I wish that Archbishop Romero were alive today, and I could hear the voice of the Father of those who are humble and oppressed. I don't think anyone who still has a heart can be indifferent to our suffering."[44]

Some of these same refugees date the beginning of their passion with the death of Romero: "Ever since Archbishop Romero died, we began to suffer; since then, we've had to flee with our children and sleep in the hills."[45] Many of those who fled to the mountains eventually crossed into Honduras to safety, but they never lost hope to return home one day to El Salvador.

In one of his homilies, Archbishop Romero spoke of the passion of the Salvadoran people as the passion of Christ:

How well Christ identifies with the suffering of our people! So many people cry out from the slums, the prisons, in their suffering and hunger for justice and peace, "My God, why have you abandoned me?" You have not abandoned us. This is the hour in which the Son of God is passing by bearing the weight of sin...from so much injustice and selfishness.[46]

Romero accompanied his people on their liberation journey. In the end, he too was engulfed by their passionate witness to life, and by the violence that sought to silence the prophetic voices — his and theirs. But his word has not been silenced; on the contrary, like the blood of the martyrs, his faithfulness unto death is his most eloquent word.

Even when they call us mad, when they call us subversives and Communists, and all the epithets they put on us, we know that we only teach the subversive witness of the Beatitudes, which have turned everything upside down to proclaim "Blessed are the poor, blessed are those who thirst for justice, blessed are those who suffer."[47]

As the memory of Jesus was alive in the first generation of Christians, many of whom had known Jesus personally, the memory of Oscar Romero is alive in his people. And as the early Christian communities bore witness to the Spirit of the risen Christ in their midst, the poor in El Salvador continue to offer us the key to Romero's spirituality, a spirituality which, in its depths, bears witness to that same Spirit of the risen Christ:

The secret of Monseñor Romero is simply that he resembled Jesus, and in our days he continues to make Jesus present to us. He witnesses to the Witness.... And for that reason the eyes of many people are fixed on him, in the same way as the Letter to the Hebrews tells us to keep our eyes fixed on Jesus.[48]

Despite the violence of the war and the sacrifices that it required of the poor, thousands of Salvadorans continued to be "messengers and prophets" through the pastoral work of accompaniment, inspired by Romero's example.

Let each one of you, in your own vocation — nun, married person, bishop, priest, high-school or university student, workman, laborer, market woman — each one in your own place live the faith intensely and feel that in your surroundings you are a true microphone of God.[49]

José, the father of five children and a lay catechist, offered this testimony:

Monseñor Romero was a person who listened to the voice of God and proclaimed the Word, announcing the reign of God and denouncing injustice. . . . He was a humble person, humane and sincere. He was a bishop, but he considered himself to be the most humble of all persons. He was the pastor who most demonstrated the spirit of Christ, because Christ was the one who opened himself to the poor, to people in need, and distanced himself from the palaces of the powerful. Romero left a lesson to all who follow him: to leave behind our privileges and to value the poor.[50]

On the occasion of the anniversary of Romero's martyrdom, refugees who remembered Romero recalled that he was the one who opened the doors of the archdiocesan seminary to them just weeks before he was killed. Years later, from the grounds of that same seminary, these refugees shared their memory of Romero:

Monseñor Romero was a light for all of us who are poor, the one who guided us on our path. He was a sincere and loyal pastor who loved his people, especially those of us most in need. His life and his works demonstrated his faith and his truth. His words encouraged us to follow in his footsteps.[51]

The spirit of Oscar Romero among the poor is life-giving, and it has become a source of hope as well for the future:

> We feel that Monseñor Romero helps us when we pray. Even though they destroyed his body, they could not take his life away. We feel that he lives in our people, that his hand is over us, that he continues to attend to our cry. We have faith that his word strengthens us, and by the power of God and our own efforts we are going to work for justice and build the reign of God that he announced.[52]

Those who worked closely with Archbishop Romero regard his memory as both good news and challenge. Five years after Romero's death, Jon Sobrino was asked why Romero continues to be alive among his people. Sobrino replied: "Monseñor Romero had a great love, an immense love for his people, and for that reason he continues to live among the poor." At the University of Louvain in Belgium, where Romero had given his last address, Sobrino added:

> To those who ignore the tragedy of the poor, Monseñor Romero keeps saying, "Don't forget the millions of children of God who continue to suffer in this world." To those who offer solidarity to the poor, he gives encouragement and thanks. To all of us, Monseñor Romero continues to offer both good news and challenge.[53]

The first public procession in San Salvador in memory of Archbishop Romero's martyrdom occurred five years after his death. By then, the repression in the streets had subsided sufficiently for the people to process through the city of San Salvador to the celebration of the Mass at the cathedral where Romero's tomb is located. Still, the people's decision to openly celebrate the life of Oscar Romero was a risk. The army was ever present and threatening with rifles slung on their shoulders. Once again, Romero's spirit and his words continued to give life to the poor whose lives were at risk. The very symbols of the procession spoke to the heart of his spirituality:

A huge banner was carried at the beginning of the procession: "If they kill me, I will rise in the Salvadoran people." Behind the banner was an immense photograph of Monseñor Romero, ten feet high...and behind the photograph a river of people overflowing the streets of San Salvador — streets filled with the echoes of popular protests and bathed in blood....People sang and repeated his words: "We must demand at the very least respect for what is of greatest value: life." "In the name of God, I ask you, stop the repression!"[54]

As people drew near to the steps of the cathedral, they met the crowd inside overflowing into the streets. A long line of peasants and workers continued to process to the steps, their eyes shining, as they proudly held up pictures of Oscar Romero, their beloved pastor. One of the mothers whose son had been captured and disappeared by the death squads spoke to the crowd gathered on the steps. A sea of faces — of children, young people, elderly, all reflecting the same suffering and hope — shone in the sunlight.

Throughout El Salvador, there are many gardens of Gethsemane where the poor pass their hour of agony in prayer, sweating blood; and there are many Golgothas where the poor continue to be crucified. Precisely there, where the cross of the poor is to be found, the spirit of Oscar Romero is most present. The spirit of Romero, as the spirit of the martyrs before him, brings us back to the paschal mystery. As another refugee testified:

> When they killed Monseñor Romero, we were very sad because we thought everything had ended. But later we saw that his spirit gave us strength to resist oppression. For that reason we also believe more now in Jesus Christ.[55]

For many more years Romero's spirit enabled the poor to hold on. On the side of an adobe house in Chalatenango whose collapsed walls and fallen roof bear witness to the ravages of war, a poster was tacked. It pictured Romero, walking among his people, in one of his frequent visits to the slums of San Salvador. Below, his prophetic words encouraged refugees as they fled through the mountains to safety: "The Good Shepherd does not want security as long as security is not given to his flock."

And on the walls of the prison in Mariona, where hundreds were held without due process during the worst years of the repression, a huge mural portraying the death of Romero could be found, offering hope to those who were condemned to torture and death. There one prisoner gave testimony of Romero's presence: "This mural is the symbol for us of one who dies out of love for his people." Another prisoner added, "Monseñor Romero is like a Salvadoran Jesus Christ."[56]

Archbishop Romero's tomb is located in the cathedral, a gigantic building in the heart of San Salvador. Romero had a special affection for the cathedral, where thousands of Salvadorans crowded together each Sunday to hear his homily and to celebrate Mass. Today, as they have every day since his death in 1980, the poor come to Archbishop Romero's tomb with their flowers and their prayers, their toil and their longings. Cards with inscriptions and petitions lie near the tomb. Most are simple pieces of paper with letters scribbled on them. Some are decorated with colored paper and handwritten; others are printed with letters cut from a newspaper.

Many of the inscriptions express gratitude for the "miracle" or favor directly attributed to his intercession. Others are petitions for the conversion of a family member, or for protection on a journey to be undertaken. Many address Romero in a personal way: "Dear Monseñor. Each day that passes we feel your absence more keenly, and we understand more your greatness and your devotion to us, the poor, and to your people. We feel blessed to have known you; we will never abandon you, but always remain faithful to your memory."

Romero's assassination was ignored by the powerful during the war and largely forgotten by most ecclesiastical authorities in El Salvador. But the poor have never forgotten him. As one inscription says, "They killed you because you were with us, the poor. They tried to eliminate us, but you have not died. You live on in our struggle."

The people are certain that Romero is a saint, a certainty rooted in their intimate knowledge of one who — like thousands of other Salvadorans — generously offered his life out of love for his friends.[57] In the words of the popular ballad:

> March 24, the church will never forget; once again they bathed in blood one who spoke the truth....
>
> Today they took from us the most valiant person of the church, because of his example and courage, a true prophet....
>
> Oscar Arnulfo Romero, you were our pastor, and in the simple and humble you placed your heart....
>
> We remember when you came to our villages to see the peasants, to see your people who are poor....
>
> The blood that you shed was for the cause of a people who suffer great repression, on account of the rich and the government....
>
> It's clear to the people that your death was not isolated, it was the action of imperialism and the Armed Forces....
>
> Pilate has returned to the earth, represented by the tyrant, because they assassinated you and now wash their hands....
>
> Oscar Arnulfo has not died; he lives in the struggles of his people. For that reason we will never forget your heroic example.

Perhaps the most moving testimony to the spirit of Oscar Romero occurred on the first day of peace in San Salvador, February 1, 1992. The poor came from all parts of El Salvador, streaming down the highways with no military in sight, waving their colorful handkerchiefs as bright as their smiles, many with tears in their eyes. The war was over! Who could believe it?

They came as if in a dream, pouring through the streets of San Salvador, thousands of rivulets that began in the mountains a decade before, and now twelve years later flowed into the streets of the plaza in front of the cathedral of San Salvador — renamed the Plaza of the Martyrs — to celebrate the end of the war. Their presence brought to mind the words of the Psalmist: "They went away weeping, bearing the seeds for sowing; now they come back rejoicing, carrying the sheaves" (Ps. 126:6).

The sound of Beethoven's "Ode to Joy" filled the air: "Come, sing, dream as you sing, live and dream of a new day in which all people will become brothers and sisters." People wept openly. Twelve years, twelve long years, and now the war was finally over! So much sorrow: seventy-five thousand dead, each one with a name, a hope, a dream. So much joy: as the people who had been hidden walked into the open, many reunited with loved ones they had not seen in years, some they did not know were still alive.

And there, waving above the crowd, an immense banner with a picture of Archbishop Romero hung in front of the cathedral. The banner's message was printed in bright bold script. Not Romero's words, not Romero's promise that he would rise amid the Salvadoran people. No, the words on the banner were the people's, keeping *their* promise. The inscription read: "Archbishop Romero, you have risen in your people!"

5

The Word Remains

What remains always is the invitation to conversion: to carry forward the same options that Romero made as he worked through the structures and communities of the church...to transform our country, our continent, and our world into more humane places. Conversion is also responding to the countless basic necessities of our people, always striving with hope towards that utopia, the reign of God, for which many brothers and sisters gave their lives.[1]

Two decades after the death of Oscar Romero, violence and poverty continue to take their toll on the most vulnerable and defenseless in El Salvador. Precisely for that reason, the spirit of Oscar Romero is immensely important, because it continues to proclaim good news.

The character of the violence has changed — social violence has become endemic in a society where the poor are marginalized and excluded from the fruits of a neoliberal economy — but the impact of both poverty and violence on the poor is as devastating as before, if not more so. Before, the violence touched the bodies of the poor; now it also threatens their spirit.

There are, however, signs of hope on the horizon. New social sectors have organized to win their rights as women, the urban poor, *maquiladora* workers, and peasant farmers. Disillusionment with political parties has led to a refocusing of hopes in grassroots participation and the building up of civil society as the basis for any alternative political or economic project.

Even though the war in El Salvador has ended, the following words offered by Jon Sobrino on the occasion of the tenth anniversary of Romero's martyrdom continue to ring true today:

> In El Salvador, as well as in the entire Third World...an alarming situation still exists: inhumane poverty, cruel injustice, conflict and war, repression and the violation of human rights, disillusionment with the failures of the people, and all the suffering and darkness that this brings to the majority of the people who are poor. We all know this, but unless we are willing to deepen our awareness of it we will not be able to understand the importance of Monseñor Romero and his presence among us today.
>
> On the other hand, we continue to find creativity and hope in the struggle for liberation and the generous self-sacrifice of the martyrs, brought home to us in the recent martyrdom of the Jesuits and the commemoration of Rutilio Grande, the proto-martyr of El Salvador. The poor still have the intuition and fundamental hope that Jesus is good news for them, and that a church that resembles Jesus and responds as Jesus did is also good news. Long before the church made an option for the poor, the poor made an option for the church.[2]

And while it is certainly true that the spirit of Oscar Romero and the remembrance of his words continue to be an effective and urgent voice for transformation in El Salvador, his presence extends beyond the borders of his country. He has become, again in the words of Jon Sobrino, "the most universal Christian at the end of the twentieth century":

> Monseñor Romero inspires indigenous people and peasants, African Americans and oppressed, but also intellectuals, university professors, professionals, bishops, and humble catechists. Despite the passing of years, the commemoration of Romero's life has not diminished. In times of war and in times of peace, countless human beings continue to

celebrate him. In Romero, that which is Christian and that
which is human is very present.

If this is true, then it is not at all rhetorical to affirm
that Monseñor Romero has become a "universal Christian," and perhaps the most universal Christian of our
time.... We don't say this out of any triumphalism, but
with the same humility and simplicity with which Monseñor himself spoke.... How we wish that there were more
Romeros in the world![3]

The spirit of Oscar Romero, through his memory and through
his word, continues to be a prophetic presence in El Salvador,
offering the poor the comfort that they are not alone and the
promise that things can change. His memory is a "subversive"
one; it reminds us that the world is not meant to remain in its
current state, where the poor are excluded, the hungry forgotten,
those who grieve hidden from view, and the victims blamed for
their own persecution. Rather, the poor are blessed because theirs
is the reign of God. Life, not death, will have the last word.

On the occasion of the fifteenth anniversary of Romero's
death, Gustavo Gutiérrez recalled this deeper truth of Romero's
martyrdom as he preached in the chapel of the Jesuit martyrs in
San Salvador:

We come to this Eucharist to give thanks for Monseñor Romero and for so many who have already been resurrected
with Jesus and who will continue to be resurrected.... The
martyrs remind us of Jesus' resurrection; they recall for us
the center of our faith and of our hope. We must always
remember — in communion with the martyrs — that death
does not put an end to our hopes and joys; life is the heart
of the Christian message.[4]

The force of the resurrection continues to be present in El
Salvador and, indeed, throughout the world:

*I am not afraid that our faith may depend only on the arch-
bishop's preaching; I don't think that I'm that important. I
believe that this message, which is only a humble echo of*

God's word, enters your hearts, not because it is mine, but because it comes from God.[5]

The people continue to be the prophetic voice even when there seems to be more shadow than light, more poverty and violence than hope for transformation, more death than life. But the memory of Oscar Romero has marked the poor forever, binding their passion and death to the passion and death of Jesus Christ and raising them to new life.

Ignacio Ellacuría, himself later martyred, summarized the foundation of Romero's spirituality as follows:

Monseñor Romero based his hope on two pillars: a historic pillar, which was his knowledge of his people for whom he attributed an unquenchable capacity to find solutions to their gravest difficulties, and a transcendent pillar, which was his belief that ultimately God is a God of life and not death, that the last word of reality is good and not evil. This hope not only enabled him to overcome any temptation of discouragement; it encouraged him to continue working, aware that his effort would not be in vain, regardless of how brief the time.[6]

Oscar Romero was archbishop of San Salvador for three years — from the perspective of the poor and of his friends, a time that was much too brief. But it was also a propitious moment, "an hour of grace," in which much hope was given to the poor, and much light was shed on the reality of El Salvador. With Romero, the reign of God drew near to the people of El Salvador, and the poor heard the good news that God loves them in a special way.

A preeminent sign of Romero's spirituality is how his spirit and imagination continue to live among his people and among many of us touched by the extraordinary spirit of hope that his people carry even in these postwar moments of economic desperation. Perhaps the resurrection of hope is a more demanding feat during these years of austerity and exclusion than the war years that poets called the hour of the inferno.

In the language of the Bible, we are at a crossroads, a moment of *kairos,* when the fate of the world and future generations hangs in balance. The spirit of Oscar Romero asks us in this *kairos* moment: Will you stand with the poor? Romero is not a saint only for poor Latin Americans; his voice must be "heard" in the world of the comfortable and the safe as well. *"When many give up hope, when it seems to them the nation has nowhere to go, as though it were all over, the Christian says: No, we have just begun. We are still awaiting God's grace."*[7]

Still, Romero points again and again to the poor as the locus of God's Spirit. In this sense, the poor are not the problem but the solution. That is his message for us. If you have eyes, look into the eyes of those who have become expendable. If you have ears, listen to the voice of the voiceless.

With the end of the war years El Salvador's poor no longer "speak" to the international community. Other tragedies eclipse theirs in the media. But the policies that led to their diminishment continue. Salvadorans are picking up the pieces of their shattered nation, piecing together new patterns of survival and resistance with ingenuity and determination. The global economy does not work well for the poorest people in poor countries.

It was this form of structural violence that Romero confronted:

> *I will not tire of declaring that if we really want an effective end to violence we must remove the violence that lies at the root of all violence: structural violence, social injustice, exclusion of citizens from the management of the country, repression. All of this is what constitutes the primal cause, from which the rest flows naturally.*[8]

Surely Romero's invitation to his people is meant for us as well: *"Put all your determination, all your self-giving, all your sacrifice, even to giving your lives, for the cause of the true liberation guaranteed by the one on whom God's Spirit is poured out."*[9]

His life is a witness that allows us to interrogate power and to find hope rather than despair in the face of an often dehumanizing globalization. His legacy and our challenge is to discover the idols that crush the poor in our world today and to side with them in their struggle for dignity. Romero is a twentieth-century prophet and martyr whose life is not only a symbol but a historical gift to those of us in the North who flounder for a spiritual path at the dawn of a new millennium.

Romero was great-hearted because he allowed the poor to change his heart. We have no public consensus, not even a moral consensus among people of faith, that identifies injustice or racism as the cause of poverty. We have no social analysis that helps us see that the poor and people of color are targets, not for torture and assassination, but for exclusion and expendability. As labor no longer needed in a transformed global economy, they are blamed for their own impoverishment. To believe in the poor is a deeply spiritual, and a profoundly political, act of faith.

Romero evokes our capacity to imagine a God who is historically present in our culture, speaking from the alleys, barrios, shelters, jails, drug houses, foster homes, and skid rows. He calls us to live, to organize, to speak out and speak back, to join, to accompany whatever pockets of hope, cultural resistance, justice and peace that people make.

Social justice and a redistribution of wealth are measures of our hope. We must be creative, with audacious hope, to fashion a world without the structural violence of poverty, without cultures that exclude people, without foreign policies drenched in blood and manipulation.

The day before Romero was killed he ordered the military to stop their murderous campaign against his people. As he spoke, his voice rose above the irruptive applause with a force and clarity that shook his small frame. Forgotten, often, are his pastoral words in that historic homily. He quietly reminded the people of the radiantly alive God who would remain with them regardless of the army's brutality. *"God's reign,"* he said, *"is already present on our earth in mystery."*

In a country so filled with the mystery of inequity and evil, Oscar Romero became in death as he had been in life, a witness to the Gospel he proclaimed and its lasting hope to the poor: "The Word remains, and that Word is Life."

Notes

Introduction

1. James R. Brockman, comp. and trans., *The Church Is All of You: Thoughts of Archbishop Oscar Romero* (Minneapolis: Winston Press, 1984), 69.

2. Jenny Pearce, *Under the Eagle* (Boston: South End Press, 1981), 209.

3. Oscar Romero, *The Violence of Love,* comp. and trans. James R. Brockman (Farmington, Pa.: Plough Publishing House, 1998), 4.

4. Ibid., 87–88.

5. Brockman, *The Church Is All of You,* 25.

6. Romero, *The Violence of Love,* 121.

7. *La voz de los sin voz* (San Salvador: UCA Editores, 1987), March 19, 1980 interview, 438.

8. Archbishop Oscar Romero, "The Political Dimension of the Faith from the Perspective of the Option for the Poor," *Voice of the Voiceless: The Four Pastoral Letters and Other Statements* (Maryknoll, N.Y.: Orbis Books, 1985), 178.

1. The Centrality of the Poor

1. Equipo de Educación Maíz, *Monseñor Romero: El pueblo es mi profeta* (San Salvador: Equipo de Educación Maíz, 1994), 62.

2. Gustavo Gutiérrez, *On Job* (Maryknoll, N.Y.: Orbis Books, 1992), 96–97.

3. Archbishop Oscar Romero, "The Political Dimension of the Faith from the Perspective of the Option for the Poor," *Voice of the Voiceless: The Four Pastoral Letters and Other Statements* (Maryknoll, N.Y.: Orbis Books, 1985), 185.

4. Ibid.

5. *La voz de los sin voz* (San Salvador: UCA Editores, 1987), March 19, 1980 interview, 461.

6. Oscar Romero, *The Violence of Love,* comp. and trans. James R. Brockman (Farmington, Pa.: Plough Publishing House, 1998), 173.

7. Ibid., 72.

8. Ibid., 24.

9. Ibid., 133.

10. María López Vigil, *Piezas para un retrato* (San Salvador: UCA Editores, 1993), 75.

11. Jon Sobrino, *Archbishop Romero: Memories and Reflections* (Maryknoll, N.Y.: Orbis Books, 1990), 5.

12. López Vigil, *Piezas para un retrato,* 95.

13. Sobrino, *Archbishop Romero,* 10.

14. Ibid., 8.

15. Ibid., 9–10.

16. Archbishop Oscar Romero, *A Shepherd's Diary,* trans. Irene Hodgson (Cincinnati: St. Anthony Messenger Press, 1996), 125.

17. Equipo de Educación Maíz, *Monseñor Romero: El pueblo es mi profeta,* 11.

18. Romero, *A Shepherd's Diary,* 408.

19. Romero, *Voice of the Voiceless,* 73.

20. Ibid., 137–38.

21. James R. Brockman, *Romero: A Life* (Maryknoll, N.Y.: Orbis Books, 1989), 13.

22. *Monseñor Oscar A. Romero: Su pensamiento,* Publicaciones Pastorales Arzobispado, 8 vols. (San Salvador: Imprenta Criterio, 1980–1989), March 20, 1977 homily, vol. 1–2, 8.

23. Ibid., March 14, 1977 homily, vol. 1–2, 1.

24. Romero, *A Shepherd's Diary,* 321.

25. Ibid., 355.

26. Brockman, *Romero,* 14–17.

27. Sobrino, *Archbishop Romero,* 15.

28. Ibid.

29. *Monseñor Oscar A. Romero: Su pensamiento,* November 26, 1978 homily, vol. 5, 327.

30. Romero, *The Violence of Love,* 162.

31. Romero, *A Shepherd's Diary,* 274.

32. Photographer Jim Harney's reflections on the experience of hearing Romero preach.

33. Romero, *Voice of the Voiceless,* 179.

34. Romero, *The Violence of Love,* 173.

35. Sobrino, *Archbishop Romero,* 58.

36. *Monseñor Oscar A. Romero: Su pensamiento,* April 7, 1977 homily, vol. 1–2, 12.

37. Ibid., 14.

38. Ibid., April 8, 1977 homily, vol. 1–2, 20.

39. Ibid., May 8, 1977 homily, vol. 1–2, 29.

40. Ibid., May 12, 1977 homily, vol. 1–2, 39.

41. Ibid., June 19, 1977 homily, vol. 1–2, 97.

42. Ibid., 98.

43. Ibid., 101.

44. Romero, *The Violence of Love*, 43–44.

45. Ibid., 102.

2. The Historical Demands of the Gospel

1. Archbishop Oscar Romero, *Voice of the Voiceless: The Four Pastoral Letters and Other Statements* (Maryknoll, N.Y.: Orbis Books, 1985), 179.

2. Ibid., 179–80.

3. Oscar Romero, *The Violence of Love*, comp. and trans. James R. Brockman (Farmington, Pa.: The Plough Publishing House, 1998), 192.

4. Ibid., 136.

5. Romero, *Voice of the Voiceless*, 180.

6. Ibid., 180.

7. *Monseñor Oscar A. Romero: Su pensamiento*, Publicaciones Pastorales Arzobispado, 8 vols. (San Salvador: Imprenta Criterio, 1980–89), September 3, 1978 homily. See also Miguel Cañada Diez, *Predicación y profecía: Análisis de las homilías de Monseñor Romero* (San Salvador: UCA Editores, 1993), Masters Thesis.

8. *Monseñor Oscar A. Romero: Su pensamiento*, July 8, 1979 homily, vol. 7, 61.

9. Ibid., July 16, 1978 homily.

10. Archbishop Oscar Romero, *A Shepherd's Diary*, trans. Irene B. Hodgson (Cincinnati: St. Anthony Messenger Press, 1996), 131–32.

11. Jon Sobrino, *Archbishop Romero: Memories and Reflections* (Maryknoll, N.Y.: Orbis Books, 1990), 31.

12. Romero, *Voice of the Voiceless*, 180–81.

13. *Monseñor Oscar A. Romero: Su pensamiento*, November 11, 1979 homily, vol. 7, 421.

14. Ibid., May 21, 1978 homily, vol. 4, 258.

15. Ibid., August 28, 1977 homily, vol. 1–2, 192.

16. Ibid., January 27, 1980 homily, vol. 8, 184.

17. Ibid., 193.

18. Romero, *Voice of the Voiceless*, 181.

19. Ibid., 185.

20. Ibid., 184.

21. Ibid., 184–85.

22. *Monseñor Oscar A. Romero: Su pensamiento*, January 27, 1980 homily, vol. 8, 202.

23. Romero, *Voice of the Voiceless*, 185.

24. *Monseñor Oscar A. Romero: Su pensamiento*, September 16, 1979 homily, vol. 7, 261.

25. Romero, *Voice of the Voiceless*, 183.

26. *Carta a las Iglesias* (San Salvador: UCA Editores, 1981–), no. 20.

27. Renny Golden, *The Hour of the Poor, The Hour of Women: Salvadoran Women Speak* (New York: Crossroad, 1991), 53.

28. Ibid., 51.

29. Ibid., 54.

30. Romero, *Voice of the Voiceless*, 97.

31. Ibid., 98.

32. Ibid., 100.

33. Ibid., 105.

34. Bill Hutchinson, *When the Dogs Ate Candles: A Time in El Salvador* (Boulder: University Press of Colorado, 1998), 73.

35. Ibid., 74.

36. Ibid., 51.

37. Ibid., 64.

38. Romero, *The Violence of Love*, 101.

39. Ibid., 109.

40. Hutchinson, *When the Dogs Ate Candles*, 199.

41. Ibid., 212.

42. Romero, *Voice of the Voiceless*, 138.

43. Romero, *The Violence of Love*, 35.

44. Ibid., 35.

45. Ibid., 152.

3. The Heart of the Poor

1. Oscar Romero, *The Violence of Love*, comp. and trans. James R. Brockman (Farmington, Pa.: Plough Publishing House, 1998), 189.

2. Ibid., 163.

3. *Carta a las Iglesias* (San Salvador: UCA Editores, 1981–), no. 4.

4. *Monseñor Oscar A. Romero: Su pensamiento*, Publicaciones Pastorales Arzobispado, 8 vols. (San Salvador: Imprenta Criterio, 1980–1989), January 7, 1979 homily, vol. 6, 106.

5. Archbishop Oscar Romero, *Voice of the Voiceless: The Four Pastoral Letters and Other Statements* (Maryknoll N.Y., Orbis Books, 1985), 155.

6. *Carta a las Iglesias*, no. 10.

7. *Monseñor Oscar A. Romero: Su pensamiento*, November 18, 1979 homily, vol. 7, 445.

8. Romero, *The Violence of Love*, 91.

9. *Carta a las Iglesias*, no. 0.

10. Romero, *The Violence of Love*, 191.

11. Renny Golden, *The Hour of the Poor, The Hour of Women: Salvadoran Women Speak* (New York: Crossroad, 1991), 42–43.

12. Romero, *The Violence of Love*, 105.

13. Archbishop Oscar Romero, *A Shepherd's Diary*, trans. Irene B. Hodgson (Cincinnati: St. Anthony Messenger Press, 1993), 322.

14. Romero, *The Violence of Love*, 199.

15. *Carta a las Iglesias*, no. 31.

16. Romero, *The Violence of Love*, 27.

17. *Monseñor Oscar A. Romero: Su pensamiento*, March 16, 1980 homily, vol. 8, 348.

18. *Monseñor Oscar A. Romero: Su pensamiento*, vol. 3, 14–15.

19. James R. Brockman, comp. and trans., *The Church Is All of You: Thoughts of Archbishop Oscar Romero* (Minneapolis: Winston Press, 1984), 110.

20. Romero, *The Violence of Love*, 135.

21. Romero, *A Shepherd's Diary*, 229.

22. Ibid., 69.

23. Ibid., 238.

24. Ibid., 52.

25. Ibid., 522.

26. Ibid., 498.

27. Romero, *The Violence of Love*, 162.

28. Ibid., 136.

29. Ibid., 104.

30. James Alison, *Raising Abel: The Recovery of the Eschatological Imagination* (New York.: Crossroad, 1996), 90–91.

31. Ibid., 161–65.

4. The Testimony of the Martyrs

1. Archbishop Oscar Romero, *Voice of the Voiceless: The Four Pastoral Letters and Other Statements* (Maryknoll: N.Y.: Orbis Books, 1985), 181.

2. Carolyn Forche, "Oscar Romero," in *Martyrs*, ed. Susan Bergman (Maryknoll, N.Y.: Orbis Books, 1998), 73.

3. Oscar Romero, *The Violence of Love*, comp. and trans. James R. Brockman (Farmington, Pa.: Plough Publishing House, 1998), 146–47.

4. *Monseñor Oscar A. Romero: Su pensamiento,* Publicaciones Pastorales Arzobispado, 8 vols. (San Salvador: Imprenta Criterio, 1980–1989), June 24, 1979 homily, vol. 7, 27.

5. Jon Sobrino, *Archbishop Romero: Memories and Reflections* (Maryknoll, N.Y.: Orbis Books, 1990), 38.

6. Romero, *Voice of the Voiceless,* 182.

7. *La voz de los sin voz* (UCA), March 1980, 461.

8. Romero, *The Violence of Love,* 97.

9. *Monseñor Oscar A. Romero: Su pensamiento,* December 17, 1978 homily, vol. 6, 41.

10. *Carta a las Iglesias* (San Salvador: UCA Editores, 1981–), no. 1.

11. *La voz de los sin voz* (UCA), 461.

12. Romero, *The Violence of Love,* 175.

13. *La voz de los sin voz* (UCA), March 1980, 461.

14. Romero, *The Violence of Love,* 196–97.

15. Ibid., 142.

16. *Archbishop Oscar Romero: A Shepherd's Diary,* trans. Irene B. Hodgson (Cincinnati: St. Anthony Messenger Press, 1996), 482.

17. Ibid., 435.

18. *Monseñor Oscar A. Romero: Su pensamiento,* January 6, 1980 homily, vol. 8, 130.

19. Romero, *A Shepherd's Diary,* 452.

20. *Monseñor Oscar A. Romero: Su pensamiento,* January 27, 1980 homily, vol. 8, 193.

21. Romero, *A Shepherd's Diary,* 491.

22. Ibid., 493.

23. Ibid., 515.

24. Romero, *The Violence of Love,* 127–28.

25. *La voz de los sin voz* (UCA), March 23, 1980 homily, 291.

26. James R. Brockman, S.J., *Romero: A Life* (Maryknoll N.Y.: Orbis Books, 1989), 223.

27. Ibid., 244.

28. Ibid.

29. Roque Dalton, "Like You," in *Poetry Like Bread,* ed. Martin Espada (Willimantic, Conn.: Curbstone Press, 1994), 101.

30. *Monseñor Oscar A. Romero: Su pensamiento,* March 24, 1980 homily, vol. 8, 383–84.

31. *Carta a las Iglesias,* no. 92.

32. Sobrino, *Archbishop Romero,* 41.

33. "A Pastor's Last Homily," *Sojourners Magazine* (May 1980): 12, translation of Romero's March 23, 1980 homily, reprinted with permission from *Sojourners.*

34. Ibid., 12–13.

35. Ibid., 14.

36. Romero, *The Violence of Love*, 98.

37. "A Pastor's Last Homily," 15.

38. Ibid., 15–16.

39. *La voz de los sin voz,* March 1980 interview, 461.

40. *Carta a las Iglesias,* no. 206.

41. Ibid.

42. Ibid.

43. Ibid.

44. Ibid., no. 24.

45. Ibid., no. 28.

46. *Monseñor Oscar A. Romero: Su pensamiento,* November 11, 1979.

47. Romero, *The Violence of Love*, 48.

48. *Carta a las Iglesias,* 48.

49. James R. Brockman, comp. and trans., *The Church Is All of You: Thoughts of Archbishop Oscar Romero* (Minneapolis: Winston Press, 1984), 105.

50. *Carta a las Iglesias,* no. 53.

51. Ibid., no. 64.

52. Ibid., no. 64.

53. Ibid., no. 85.

54. Ibid., no. 88.

55. Ibid., no. 89.

56. Ibid., no. 128.

57. Ibid., no. 16.

5. The Word Remains

1. *Carta a las Iglesias* (San Salvador: UCA Editores, 1981–), no. 302.

2. Ibid., no. 206.

3. Ibid., no. 254.

4. Ibid., no. 326.

5. Oscar Romero, *The Violence of Love*, comp. and trans. James R. Brockman (Farmington, Pa.: Plough Publishing House, 1998), 98.

6. *Carta a las Iglesias,* no. 350.

7. Romero, *The Violence of Love*, 158.

8. Ibid., 166.

9. Ibid., 186.

MODERN SPIRITUAL MASTERS SERIES

Other volumes in this series are available at your local bookseller
or directly through Orbis Books.

Dietrich Bonhoeffer
Writings Selected with an Introduction by Robert Coles
ISBN 1-57075-194-3, paperback

Charles de Foucauld
Writings Selected with an Introduction by Robert Ellsberg
ISBN 1-57075-244-3, paperback

Anthony de Mello
Writings Selected with an Introduction by William Dych
ISBN 1-57075-283-4, paperback

Henri Nouwen
Writings Selected with an Introduction by Robert A. Jonas
ISBN 1-57075-197-8, paperback

Pierre Teilhard de Chardin
Writings Selected with an Introduction by Ursula King
ISBN 1-57075-248-6, paperback

Simone Weil
Writings Selected with an Introduction by Eric O. Springsted
ISBN 1-57075-204-4, paperback

For a free catalog or to place your order with Mastercard
and VISA, call toll-free 1-800-258-5838,

E-mail via our Web page at http://www.maryknoll.org/orbis

or write to: **ORBIS BOOKS**
Walsh Building, P.O. Box 302
Maryknoll, N.Y. 10545-0302

Thank you for reading *Oscar Romero.*
We hope you enjoyed it.